Living Beyond Fate

Wesley N. Wietgrefe

Produced by GWW Books

Rapid City, South Dakota

GWW Books, 1811 Sunny Springs Dr., Rapid City, South Dakota 57702
Website: www.RelatingtoAncients.com   Email: gwwbooks@outlook.com

Ordering Information *Quantity sales.* Special discounts are available on quantity purchases by schools, book clubs, organizations, businesses, and others. Submit a request at www.RelatingtoAncients.com, or gwwbooks@outlook.com.

Print credits: *Book production:* GWW Books, Rapid City, SD. *Photos*: Wesley N. Wietgrefe collection

Font: Garamond

Name: Wietgrefe, Wesley N., 1957— author.

Title: Living Beyond Fate

Wesley N. Wietgrefe, Henderson, Nevada

Identifiers: Paperback ISBM 979-8-9881736-4-9.

Subjects: Nonfiction: Memoir — Entertainment -- Spirituality

Classification: BISAC Codes: 1. REGIONAL THEME 4.0.1.4.11.0.0 North America/USA/States/South Dakota; 2. BIO 0038000 Biography & Autobiography/Survival

First Edition. First Printing. Printed in United States of America.

Dedicated to my wife, children, grandchildren, sister, and brothers.

Contents

Acknowledgements

I want to thank my whole family with special acknowledgement to those who directly assisted with this project:

Gary Wietgrefe, my oldest brother, helped me format and publish through his self-publishing business, GWW Books. Additional copies of this book can be ordered through his website https://www.RelatingToAncients.com/. I'm not sure if I would have followed through to the end on this project without his strong support.

Thank you Susan and Rob Boyer, my sister and brother-in-law, who proofread one of my first drafts.

I call on my wife Jeanne for many things including collaborating stories with me and using her abilities to find errors by proofing. This was not fun for her, but she endured trying to help me with my punctuation and spelling.

My son Wade has continued to encourage me to gather these many stories in one document. My daughter, son-in-law, and wonderful grandchildren give me constant pride.

Without my entire family, I would not have so many family photos to use to remind me of details. My family also verified many details through conversations. They unknowingly supported my efforts to put these stories in writing.

Introduction

Though I have authored ten books, brother Wesley is much more succinct with his entertaining anecdotes.

Everyone has life stories. They all differ. Since birth we experience things that can kill us—we tend to forget them. Remarkable ones we cannot forget. Wesley entertains readers with life's struggles, happenstances, and death-defying acts.

Some say we survive incidents by luck or experience. I would suggest it is by Divine guidance. Over the years, my brother, Wesley, had far more split-second stories than us other six siblings combined.

Those that boast generally exaggerate. Not my brother Wesley. If anything, over the last few decades, when we have asked him to detail life-and-death tales, he nonchalantly summarizes well-known stories of his youth. When pressed, we continually learn things he did on our South Dakota farm, some before he was school-age, many, many more thereafter. It became a trend. Why did he live? Only God knows!

Seven decades have provided fond family memories, but some of Wesley's stories herein were new to me. As U.S. novelist, Pearl Buck (1892-1973) wrote *"Ah well, perhaps one has to be very old before one learns how to be amused rather than shocked."*

My brother's stories may amuse and shock you.

Gary W. Wietgrefe

x

Living Beyond Fate

I am going to tell you a little history of my life. My family and others have told me to get these written down.

I survived many times where I probably should not have lived. For those that do not believe in God and Guardian Angeles, I want to tell you that I strongly believe.

Wes Wietgrefe

This is a photo of our farmstead taken a half mile away. We grew up in the semi-arid Plains of northern South Dakota. The land is flat, flat, flat, and there are few trees. Do not be fooled. What may be flat and boring to some is dangerous to others like me.

All photos are from our family collection.

Starting Out

In 1957, I was born in Aberdeen, South Dakota, the fifth of seven children. My parents were Walter Fred Wietgrefe Jr. and Bernice Betrice Wietgrefe (Berg).

I am far right.

When I arrived, my one sister, Susan, was age five and my oldest sibling. My brothers: Gary age four, Mark age three, Wayne age two.

We all lived in a small farmhouse--smaller than most people's garages. The size of this house was 18 by 20 feet with 360 square foot living space.

The house had a bedroom, and kitchen/living room. There was a dugout space under the house used for storing canned goods.

We had an outhouse for our bathroom needs. The kitchen sink did have running water, which was a plus. I was too young to remember living in that house, but I do remember we were happy kids.

Two more boys, Neal and Kent, were born after me.

In that tiny house (as they call homes of this size today) my parents would help relatives and friends from time to time having an extra child or two, stay with us.

All the children slept in the living room. You may be able to tell, my parents were not wealthy people by any means.

My grandparents lived a half mile away on the main farmstead in a two-story house. That house, at that time, did not have an entryway. The main level had a bedroom, kitchen, pantry with a dining, living room and a bathroom.

The upstairs consisted of two large bedrooms with a steep staircase running up the middle of the house separating the two rooms. The stairs ended with a landing that was big enough to have space to add a closet for the two rooms.

Day Vacation

Vacation for our family was a day of fishing.

When I was three years old, my family and the Schweninger family, who are relatives of ours, were fishing together at what I believe to be the Minnesota River in Montevideo, Minnesota.

I was out playing in the park area. Monte Schweninger and my Mother saw me running and falling into the water. The current was strong with the water moving me swiftly downstream.

Monte, with no regard for his own safety, jumped into the river and caught me before I drowned.

Dad, who was further upstream, quickly came running and helped pull both of us back on shore.

Mom said she was so scared that both of us would drown. She always highly respected Monte for his quick actions.

This was the first time that I survived what could have been death for me.

Background

My father stayed on the farm mainly to help my grandparents to stay afloat--keeping the farm going. My grandfather was crippled from a car accident in 1936 or 1937.

My father had to quit high school to help on the farm. In those years farming was extremely labor intensive--using horses for all the tractor uses that came later.

Pitch forks were used for stacking hay and many other chores.

My father also milked cows and fed all the livestock by hand daily--year-round. For those that do not know, doing farm chores year-round in South Dakota there are a lot of weather changes throughout the year.

Freezing cold December, January, and February brought temperatures reaching negative 30 degrees or more. Wind chill temperatures would feel like 60 below zero. The summer temperatures reached over 100 degrees Fahrenheit with often eighty percent or more humidity.

I always looked at my father as a notably big man. He had very thick, rough big hands from all the arduous work and from freezing them several times throughout the years.

Dad's wedding band I could drop a quarter through it without touching the sides. I have never met anyone with that big of hands to this day. The size of his hands always amazed me as a penny fits inside of my wedding band.

Climbing

When I was just old enough to crawl, my mother and siblings were kept busy looking after me as I liked to climb. I climbed on anything I could.

Of course, I don't remember doing that but was told that while we were at my grandparents' house, when I was a little over a year old I was found on top of the upright piano.

The piano was around five-foot high, and I was yelling HELP ME! I didn't know how to get down yet.

As I got older, I was always climbing trees and anything else I could.

My Aunt Geraldine (moms youngest sister) recently told of a story of her memory of me when she was visiting our farm.

Everyone was looking for me. I was around the age of four. She said they searched for me for some time until she heard a laugh from above her in a tree.

She said that I was hanging from my legs about fifteen feet above her. I made her so nervous that she did not want to scare me because if I were to have fallen from that height, she said she did not know what would have happened.

She recently told me that mom had told her that I was the daredevil child in the family. I confirmed it to her.

Homemade Parachute

I was around six or seven when I had watched a television show with men jumping out of a plane with parachutes.

I thought that was what I wanted to do someday. I couldn't wait for someday to come so I planned to make my own parachute.

I waited until the day when mom went to Aberdeen to grocery shop. She took Gary, Mark, and Wayne with her.

Dad was at work in town and Susan was left to keep an eye on me and Neal.

While Susan was playing with Neal, I snuck out of the house with a bed sheet in hand. I climbed the fence next to the barn where the roof slanted down on the milking side of the barn. I threw the sheet on the roof and pulled myself up on the roof. I then climbed to the top of the roof.

I figured I needed to be that high for the parachute to work. I grabbed the four corners of the sheet and jumped.

All I can say is that the sheet must have worked somewhat as I didn't kill myself or break anything. I did hit the ground hard enough to make me black and blue all over.

Once I got up, I noticed that I tore the sheet a little. I hurried back to the house and put the sheet on the ground under the clothesline. So, Susan would think it fell off.

Susan had been washing that morning and the clothesline already had bedding hanging on it. I did not tell anyone what I did till I was much older.

I decided parachuting was not a good plan for my future.

The Auger

I do remember one time I climbed up on our grain auger that was six-inches in diameter, and I think sixteen-feet-long. I think I was around five or six years old.

I started pulling out a sparrow nest from the top end of the auger. The auger was not attached to anything. My weight was too much to keep it up in the air. I was approximately twelve feet high.

The top of the auger tipped down to the ground with a clump. I slipped off the top end with the sparrow nest falling all over me.

The nest was full of lice. Lice crawled all over me. I was injured from the fall, but the lice were what really scared me.

I worried that I had broken the grain auger when the feeder end fell back to the ground with a big crunching sound.

The noise alerted mom as she was outside hanging laundry on the clothesline. She came running toward me as she thought that I had really gotten hurt.

I told her I had lice all over me and she immediately stripped off my clothes and told me to run over to the garden where the garden hose was laying.

She sprayed me off. That water was very cold. She grabbed a towel from the clothesline wrapping me up. She then carried me into the house and put me in the bathtub.

It was rare for me to bath in a tub of clean water and have soap suds all over. The warm water and suds killed the remaining lice.

While it was scary to have had all those lice on me, I did really enjoy that bath. Most of the time I had to bathe after my oldest brothers had their baths and bathed with my brother Wayne. The water was never very clean by the time we got in.

The auger was fine, just bent the metal a little on the end. I did not get a spanking but did get a good scolding and was told never to do that again.

Corn sheller

We had a hand crank corn sheller. It was a very simple machine where you would drop an ear of corn in a feeder end at the top of the sheller.

There was a hand crank to feed the ear of corn down through two steel plates with grinding spikes on each of the plates. The ear of corn would be crushed between these plates and the kernels of corn would break away from the corn cob. The kernels would come out of a separate chute and the cobs would fall out of another chute.

Again, being six years old, that machine fascinated me.

I was much too small to reach high enough to put the corn into the top and then turn the hand crank. I was determined that I could do it, so I took one of the five-gallon pails that were used for shelled corn and set it upside down.

I then put a few ears of corn on top of the pail leaving enough room for me to stand on the pail. I picked up my first ear of corn, put it into the top of the sheller and grabbed the crank handle.

It took me a few tries before I figured out how I could push and pull the crank handle enough to get it to go all the way around.

I had to move the pail each time so I could push the handle up and then move the pail again to pull the handle down. This worked for me for a few ears of corn, and I was feeling like a big kid at that time.

I had about a half pail filled with kernels. Then I put in a big ear that was fatter and longer than most of the others. I pushed the crank up and then gave the crank a pull, but the ear was stuck.

The handle of the crank was just past its top point, and I could not pull it down because the fat long ear was stuck.

I put my right hand into the top of the sheller and tugged on that ear of corn. I know I worked on that ear for some time before it came loose. When it did come loose the handle of the crank came down quickly and my hand went down with that fat ear of corn pulling it into the sheller.

I was lucky that it was a long ear of corn as the handle went from the top to the bottom quickly and stopped. My hand was stuck in the sheller between the spikes on the grinding plates.

I let out a scream and my oldest brother Gary, who was in the yard somewhere, came running to find me. Gary, being no older than ten at the time, worked the handle backwards and got my hand out of the sheller.

I'm sure I was screaming the entire time. Once Gary got me out, he carried me to the house running as fast as he could.

I think Mom, being home at the time, took me to the hospital in town right away. X-rays were taken of my hand. My thumb was broken in three places, which can give you somewhat of an idea of how close the spikes were on the grinding plates. My thumb was not very big at that age.

Luckily, the rest of my hand was ok. The doctor put what I thought were short popsicle sticks and a lot of tape on my thumb and around my wrist. He gave me a Lollipop and told me to stay away from the corn sheller till I was much older.

To this day the scars from the sheller are on my thumb and I have always had pain flash's go through that thumb. Something that I just got used to.

Chores

My chores as a kid were all well organized as they were for our entire family. My mother really knew how to get things accomplished around the farm as Dad worked construction.

We were taught how to work at a very young age. Starting out setting and clearing the table when we were old enough to sit at the table on our own, not in a highchair of course but I would say around three to four-years-old.

Never by ourselves but with the help of the other older brothers and my sister we set the table. Susan being the only girl in the family, did not really get to progress to the outdoor chores like us boys. Dishes were always part of her chore requirement.

Once we made the progress of doing a proper job cleaning dishes, house chores became part of our jobs. We were each assigned a room to be cleaned at first. That meant the room had to be cleaned from top to bottom every Saturday, dusting, vacuuming, and scrubbing the floor.

Mom would inspect our assigned room for organization and how well we cleaned. We always said she did a white glove dusting check even though she never wore white gloves anywhere, especially not in the house.

If the room did not meet her requirements, we each had to start all over again. Then, we had to make sure everything was done to her satisfaction, or you were not allowed to go out and play or watch tv.

Like I said, cleaning started out as a room and quickly progressed to cleaning the entire house.

Chores always came first.

My mother was tough but fair as we all had to go through the same process. I am not sure how much house cleaning Gary and Mark did as I only remember seeing them clean the entryway. They probably had to clean like the rest of us, but I just don't remember seeing them do so.

I always felt my brother Wayne and I had to clean the house more than our older brothers because we were not needed for milking and feeding the larger livestock until Gary was a junior or senior in high school.

When we were old enough to get assigned outdoor chores, we were excited. As kids, to get assigned an outdoor chore meant maturity.

However, Wayne and I had to continue with house cleaning even after we began doing the milking and taking care of the livestock.

Neal was just getting old enough to start house chores and Kent was just a baby when Susan moved to Minneapolis for lab tech school after she graduated from high school. The following year Gary left for the Air Force. Mark followed Gary into the Air Force as well (a year after Gary).

Losing three family members in three years, cleaning the house did get a little easier without so many people in the house.

Rooster

We had several kinds of livestock animals on our farm. We raised chickens for eggs to eat and sell. The chickens were also raised for our food supply, young ones for frying and older ones used for soups.

Some years we raised a bunch of chicks for fall slaughter. In those days farm wives would go to each other's farm and help each other out with butchering and packaging of the poultry. Most of the birds were canned in glass mason jars to preserve the meat for winter usage.

My mother could make all kinds of different meals from that canned chicken.

Back to the butchering: chicken heads were cut off and the chickens were dropped in a tub of boiling water. The boiling water would loosen all the feathers and a couple of ladies would pluck the feathers off.

As kids, we were also involved in this activity. After a short period of time, we would get used to killing the birds.

One particular year I remember one of the ladies brought her kids along. One was considered a hellion. He was always doing something that got himself and everyone around him in trouble. He made bets with us that the chicken could run with its head cut off.

Of course, we did not believe him.

He grabbed a chicken, cut its head off, set it on the ground and that headless bird took off running like you would not believe.

One year we had a big rooster that really ruled the roost. He was quite a large colorful bird with big colorful tail feathers, large feet with long claws. This rooster we always needed to keep an eye out for him when we went to gather eggs and feed the chickens because if you were not watching he would attack you from behind.

One day mom was out in the front yard--not sure what she was doing. That big rooster did not like it and attacked mom jumping up on her back, getting into her hair, and leaving a couple big scratches on her neck.

Anyone that really knew my mother would know she wouldn't put up with that kind of behavior.

After the rooster made his second attempt at attacking my mother, we had fried rooster that evening for dinner. I don't recall us ever getting another rooster on the farm after that.

Chicken Poop

Our first outdoor chores started off with feeding chickens and gathering eggs. If you had chickens assigned to you it was fun for the most part until it came time to clean the chicken coop.

This task was anything but fun. We always had a lot of chickens for a small farm.

For weeks we put fresh straw in laying boxes and on the floor of the chicken coop. This left a matting of wet straw (with no other way to put it); it filled with chicken poop.

Chicken poop and straw forms an ammonia smell that can really take your breath away. We always wore a bandana around our mouth and nose while cleaning the coop. We should have had a respirator instead of a bandana.

To this day I cannot stand the smell of ammonia cleaning solution as that is what chicken waste and straw smelled like but much stronger then the smell of Lysol®.

Skunk Juice

Our chickens were free to roam the farmyard and would at times lay eggs wherever they wanted. That reminds me of a couple of stories.

Once when I was out searching for chicken nests, I went into our old lean-to garage that was connected to the chicken coop. The garage was in bad shape for as long as I can remember but when I was little it was used for a lot of things.

It was our tack room for our horses' saddles and harness for when the horses worked the fields just before my time. It had dad's tools. One of the most important items on the farm was our welder. The floor was dirt and there were broken boards on the side walls. It also held the old crank corn sheller which I covered a little earlier.

Getting back to looking for a chicken nest: I was reaching under a bench and was taken by total surprise as a skunk was also going after the eggs under the bench.

That skunk sprayed me right in the face and the whole front of my body.

I ran from the garage not being able to see from the stinging and throwing up all over the place. That skunk got me good.

I stripped down and with a stick mom picked up my clothes and went directly to the burning barrel with them. In those days my folks did not have any money to burn, but those clothes had to go.

Mom was the only one brave enough to get close to me--standing naked in the yard.

Mom first sprayed me down with a garden hose and yelled at my brother Wayne to run to the basement and bring jars of tomato juice.

My mom canned vegetables every year and we had several quarts of tomato juice on hand.

Mom dumped a couple of jars of tomato juice on me and told me to scrub with it. As I did, mom showed up with the big metal wash tub and started to dump quart after quart of tomato juice in it. I got in and had my first and hopefully my last tomato juice bath.

Tomato juice cut the smell of skunk. I sure was glad of that.

My stomach hurt for days from the heaving, and I could not get myself to go into that garage again for a long time.

Free-Range Eggs

Another story involved that old garage and again I was gathering eggs.

My Sister was home from college for a visit and she brought one of her roommates with her. Susan and her friend were going to do some baking and needed some eggs.

We had just taken eggs into the Ipswich creamery to sell and did not have enough eggs for baking.

My brother Wayne and I said we would go out and find some for the girls.

We both went looking for chicken nests. Wayne found a nest in the old garage, and I found a nest in the trees. We had enough eggs for Susan.

We were excited that we had found them. Wayne washed the eggs up before handing them to Susan. Susan tapped the first egg on the counter, and it exploded like a stink bomb in the kitchen.

It was horrible and ruined whatever Susan had prepared and she was so embarrassed because her girlfriend was right there when it happened.

After this incident, there was no baking done for the next couple of days.

Hunting Adventures

That is me, at age one-and-a-half--June 1959 with one of Waynes first guns.

Hunting was my favorite pass time. It was something that I enjoyed very much, and I used it to get away from everything else that was going on.

I started hunting as early as I can remember with dad and my brothers. I pretended to hunt before I ever touched a real gun. I remember when my older brothers first received their own Daisy BB gun, I thought it was the neatest thing ever and couldn't wait till I was old enough to get my own.

All my brothers loved to hunt but I think Mark loved to hunt the most. I would go with him every chance I could or at least when he let me go with him.

Mark was a true marksman and I really looked up to him for his skills. I would try to hone up on my shooting skills any chance I could. I took every opportunity I could to go out hunting.

Spring goose migration.

Growing up on our farm my brothers and I learned how to hunt, at a very young age. We had a bb gun by the age of 6 and when we were 12, we were old enough that we could shoot the single shot 22 rifle.

We used the 22 to shoot rats, gophers, cotton tails, jack rabbits, and occasionally skunk, badger, and fox that were all found on our farm. The first three were always a threat to the farmer.

Rat Hunting

Rats were not a big problem on our farm until the city dump, which was approximately seven miles from our farm, was poisoned.

Rats left the dump in droves and caused many area farmers problems in their barns and grain bins.

I remember sitting up in the rafters of our old red grain barn in the evenings with the bb gun shooting rats.

BB's were much less expensive than 22 shells and I had less chance of getting in trouble with our folks for shooting in a building.

While rats were a big problem, I sure had fun hunting them.

Gopher Tails

Edmunds County offered five cents for each gopher tail. They were Richardson ground squirls, also known as Flicker Tails, part of the family of gophers. They were a big problem for all farmers and cattlemen. They dug holes everywhere. Each hole could cause larger animals, like cattle and horses, to accidently step in a hole and get sprained legs or broken ankles.

One summer a couple of my classmates, Mike and Tim, rode their bikes five miles out to our farm. I think we were about eight or nine-years-old at the time. They wanted to go gopher hunting with me.

Mom would not let me take the bb gun out with other kids. So, I got inventive and said OK if we can't go shooting gophers lets go fishing for gophers.

We grabbed three fishing rods and made a loop on the end of the line using the swivels already attached to the lines and put the loops around the top of the gopher holes.

We would let out a whistle and when the gopher popped their head out of the hole, we would real them in. We spent a couple of hours doing this and I let Mike and Tim take the tails home.

I am not sure if it was their story of adventure on our farm or that the ride was five miles from town, but they were not allowed to come out to our farm until a few years later.

Potassium and Gophers

One of the (unnamed) guys took potassium from the science lab when we were in the eighth grade and brought it out to our farm.

We took a pail to get water from the creek and put the potassium in a gopher hole. We dumped water down the hole and listened for the explosion and watched for the gophers to come out.

It was a lot of fun, but our punishment was not.

Michigan Pheasant Hunters

Our pheasant hunting group came from northern Michigan. Elmer, the tall man on the left was in his eighties. Ed, the man kneeling on the left with a cap on his head, was in

his late sixties or early seventies.

Elmer and Ed took a liking to me right off the get go and asked if I could ride with them hunting.

Mom was not too keen on me going hunting with them at first, being strangers to us at the beginning. But they told mom that if we cleaned the birds for them and packaged them, they would pay $3 a bird.

Mom, a businessperson, quickly did the math in her head and liked the proposal. She used that extra cash to help with bills. We would be cleaning our own birds anyway, what's a few more.

Mom decided it would be okay for me to go with Elmer and Ed as neither one of them wanted to do much walking. I would direct Elmer and Ed to the ends of fields to post or position themselves to wait for pheasants to come out. Meanwhile, the rest of the group would walk the fields.

My other brothers would walk with the other Michigan hunters through the field. All the walkers were good shooters.

I would ride with Elmer and Ed in Elmer's car. Elmer liked to drive the area around our farm. Ed did the driving from Michigan. Elmer liked chewing snus while doing so.

It was the first time I was around anyone that chewed.

Ed had me ride in the front seat with Elmer while he rode in the back seat. I think he needed a break from the snus as Michigan was a long way from our farm.

Little did I know that riding in front came with some unexpected surprises.

Like I said, Elmer chewed snus and he had a coffee can between him and me on the floorboard. Elmer would spit his snus at the coffee can. He hit the can most of the time. My left pant leg and boot were covered when he missed. It took a little time for me to get used to the snus.

Elmer supplied me with his old single shot 12-gauge shotgun, and also paid for the shells. He also bought me snacks of my choosing to go hunting with them.

Having a splat of snus on my leg every so often wasn't so bad. Walking in tall grass helped my boots and sometimes my pant leg taking most of it off. Elmers aim was not quite as good with a gun as his can spitting.

Ed knew all of this and made a deal that he would pay me a $1.00 a bird for everyone I shot for them. I surprised him as I averaged $6.00 a day. I did not dare shoot more than that or we could possibly go over our three-person bag limit of nine birds total per day.

Ed would hit at least one a day, sometimes two or three. I always left one bird just in case Elmer hit one. If he did not get one a half hour before sundown, I would have a chance to shoot the final bird, making it a $7 day.

It was great income for me at the time. I made enough money in the short time they stayed usually a week to pay for my shells for the rest of the year.

I was twelve years old going on 13 so I had my hunters safety course and was of legal age to carry a gun.

The funniest thing about using a 12-gauge shotgun that first year was I had one very sore, black and blue shoulder by the time they left.

Ed and Elmer used semi-automatic 12-gauge shot guns. They shot almost six times the shells I shot using the single shot shotgun and I hit twice as many birds.

The single shot forced me to aim better before taking the shot. I always thought semi-automatics guns in general shoot a lot more shots leaving hope to drop their targets.

Fox

One time my brother Wayne and I were out jack rabbit hunting driving our pickup around-and-around our 960 acres of fields.

Wayne was the driver, and I did most of the shooting. We scared up a fox in a stubble field and the pursuit began.

Fox can really run, and Wayne loved the chase behind the wheel.

We chased that fox back and forth across the field until we hit a dead furrow, and the truck went up on two wheels. I still don't know how Wayne was able to keep the truck from rolling over as we were up on two wheels for what seemed like at least quarter mile or more before we came back down. I'm sure it was less than that but at the time it felt a lot longer.

That was the luckiest fox we came upon over the years, the one that got away.

Both Wayne and I made a pact that we would never tell anyone what happened because if we did, we may never be able to drive or hunt again. This is the first time I mentioned this since other than talking with Wayne about it.

Jack Rabbits

Jack rabbits in the 1960s and '70s were also a huge problem for farmers at that time. There were few natural predators in the area back then.

Furriers offered twenty-five-cents per jack rabbit.

While pheasant hunting with Ed and Elmer paid for the shells, hunting jack rabbits was the main source of income for my brothers and me. Many years there were more rabbits than pheasants so shells did not last through winter rabbit hunts.

We were able to pay for our BB's, 22 shells, and occasionally pieces of store-bought candy or gum from selling jack rabbits.

We did not receive allowances like the town kids did for doing chores.

One year, I am not sure when, but I think it was 1973, we had a rabbit drive on what we call the Little Place pasture. We had somewhere between twenty-five-to-thirty people walking the pasture from the south to the north. In that half mile walk there were around eighty jack rabbits killed.

Whatever year it was Wayne and I made two trips to Bowdle (about thirty-six miles northwest of our farm on Highway 12) with two pickup boxes full of jack rabbits.

The second trip was in a blizzard on the way home, and we were not sure we were going to make it back. Wayne was what I thought to be a fearless driver at the time.

He drove through drifts of snow that I wasn't sure if we were on the road half of the time. We could not see more than five feet in front of us most of the time. But we made it back home and smiled at the money we made from selling rabbits.

Dunked in Ice

When I was around 13 years old, I went out pheasant hunting on my own. I was supposed to stay on our land.

It was in December, and the temperature was fairly nice--around 35 to 38 degrees with very light winds.

I walked our pasture creek bed that usually would scare up a few pheasants. The birds had been hunted before and would run and hide in the tall grass.

As I walked, I got one bird to fly up and I got it. As I was getting to the end of our pasture several birds flew out too far ahead of me to shoot. They flew across the road onto our neighbors pasture. We were allowed to hunt there before, and I thought I would just go across and try to get my other two birds before heading back home.

I walked to their dam. The dam was frozen over. I was going to walk across to the other side where the grass was much taller. I was about halfway across, and the ice broke with both of my legs going into 10-15 feet deep icy water.

The gun stopped me from going down further. I was able to pull myself out. At that point I knew I had to get back home as quickly as possible. Only my legs and hands got wet, and had it been any colder outside I don't think I would have made it back home.

My pant legs were stiff as a board and frozen to my legs. I could not feel my feet or hands by the time I got home.

Mom came to my rescue once again and put me in the bathtub clothes and all--except my snow boots came off.

I was very blessed by someone, once again, protecting me. Though frostbite on my toes and fingers, otherwise I was in good condition.

Whoa Not Go

One time we were out pheasant hunting in our pickup truck. Mark was driving through a wheat stubble field on our northwest quarter of land.

I believe Neal was in the cab with him, Gary, Wayne and I were all riding in the pickup box with loaded shot guns.

Gary spotted a pheasant and yelled **WHOA, WHOA** to Mark.

The three of us were getting ready to jump out of the truck box when Mark thought Gary said go, Go, GO! The three of us in the box held on for dear life with us all yelling at that point to stop.

Mark slammed on the brakes and the dust was flying everywhere. I think Gary's face was as red or redder than his hair at that point. He yelled, "What the hell were you doing? I yelled WHOA, NOT GO!" After a few minutes we were all laughing and went on hunting.

Dove Pecker

Dove hunting season was in progress. We normally did not hunt doves. Susan said she had nothing planned for dinner one evening.

Mom was in the hospital at the time and Dad was putting some very long hours at work. Mark was out in the field working. Gary, I think was in Kansas City for FFA animal judging.

Wayne and I thought we could go shoot a few doves and clean them in time for dinner. Susan was not sure she wanted to cook doves but said OK.

We went out in our shelter belt which was L shaped. Wayne went west to east in our backyard bordering the trees. I took the north to south side of the shelterbelt.

There were always a lot of doves in our trees, and we never hunted them before. There never was a need to do so. We came back a few minutes later to clean the birds.

While cleaning them we came up one bird short for the family. I said I would see if I could find one more and I will clean it and bring it in as soon as I can.

Wayne went into the house and helped Susan prepare the meal. I looked and looked and couldn't find a single dove at the time. Ok either I don't eat, or I need to shoot something else around the same size.

At that moment a flicker tail woodpecker flew in front of me. I shot that woodpecker, cleaned it right away and took it to the house.

Susan said you got a big one. She had the dove fried up with mashed potatoes and some other fresh vegetables from the garden. We all sat down with Grandpa Wietgrefe on his end of the table and the rest of us in our seating arrangement around the table.

Susan brought the batch of dove breasts to the table and sat them in front of Grandpa and Mark. I thought for sure Grandpa (who only had one tooth) was going to get the woodpecker as it was the biggest breast on the platter.

We said grace and everyone started passing the food around. Mark took the first pick of breast right away. Everyone was complimenting Susan on how good the dove was. Nobody had ever eaten dove before.

Mark said his was kind of tough but tasted ok. I started to snicker, and he knew something was up. Mark gave me a look and said," OK Wes, what was it?"

I made sure I had room to run just in case I needed to. I then told him it was a woodpecker because there were no more doves to shoot at the time. Everyone burst out laughing except for Mark. I said that is what you get for taking the biggest piece first.

Mouse Target

We had two geese and a few Muscovy ducks running around the farm. One day my older brother Mark and I were out in the (tree) shelterbelt hunting.

I remember carrying a sling shot with me at the time. I had been restricted from the BB gun at that time because a few days earlier I had shot my younger brother Neal in the chest with a bb.

What happened was Neal had caught a mouse and was holding it by the tail. I told him to hold the mouse to the side and I would shoot it out of his hand.

I believe Neal was 4 years old and I was seven at the time.

Well Neal started out holding the mouse to his left side while I was focusing my aim to shoot the mouse.

Neal got nervous and moved his hand out front of himself.

I shot hitting the mouse and bb went through the mouse and hit Neal in the chest leaving a little mark on his chest.

I don't believe it broke his skin, but it stung him good. Hence, I was restricted from using the gun for some time. I had a very sore backside for a while also.

Farmyard Goose

Back to hunting with Mark and the goose.

Mark was an excellent shot, he didn't miss his target very often with a gun, sling shot, or throwing a rock at his target. Mark should have been a baseball pitcher as he threw hard, fast, and rarely missed his target.

We were not finding anything to shoot at for some time and our very old gray and white goose showed up in front of us. Mark loved to prank people and animals sometimes. Mark with no intention of shooting the goose just wanted to scare it a little to get it out of our path.

Mark fired a bullet that hit the ground near the geese and the gray goose fell over dead. We both knew that he hadn't hit the goose with the bullet unless it bounced off the ground hitting it somehow. That really did not seem likely, and we could not figure out why the goose fell over.

This really bothered Mark and he was wondering what punishment he may receive for killing our old gray goose.

We did an autopsy to see if the bullet hit the goose. There was no bullet. The scare apparently caused the goose to have a heart attack. At least that was our conclusion.

It was an old goose after all. Mark didn't pull pranks on animals after that incident. I don't think he caught too much hell from mom when he told her what had happened. I believe the only comment that mom made was OH! MARK!

Antelope

Gary and Mark were both still on the farm when we went Antelope hunting on a very large ranch in western South Dakota.

I remember dad had to sign a document stating if we were to accidentally shoot a cow or bull on that ranch we would owe that rancher a very large amounts of money for the animal.

So, dad made it very clear to us to make sure of our aim before we went hunting. This was wide open range land with many gullies and hills.

I got on a trail of a large buck and shot. I was sure I had hit him, so I told the group I was going to track him while the others went after another group of antelopes.

I tracked after the buck for well over an hour going up and down the gullies and hills. I was getting tired and decided I would see if I could get one more shot before heading back to the group.

The buck had just climbed out a deep gully and stopped for a second. I took the shot and he dropped. He was a good hundred-and-fifty yards away and on the other side of this deep gully.

Excited I ran over to him and bled him out right away. I then stood up and looked around and could not spot my landmark. I got really concerned at that point as there was no way anyone could drive to my location, and I really was not sure where I was at.

I decided to climb the next hill and look for my landmark. I spotted it and a little relief hit me, but it looked a lot further away than I remembered.

I knew the way back, but how I was going to get that nice buck back. I gutted the antelope, tied its legs together using my belt and lifted it on my back along with my rifle strap around my neck.

This worked but my pants would not stay up.

I took the carrying strap off my gun, and belt off the legs. I put my belt back in my pants and used the gun strap to tie the legs back up.

I carried that buck up and down through the gullies while watching for rattle snakes. Each time I made it to the other side I would stop and make sure I was still on the right track back keeping the landmark insight.

I was just about ready to give up carrying the buck back and just leave it until I got help. I knew I was still a long way away from the truck.

While I sat down resting, Gary popped his head out over the hill ahead of me. Relief ran through my body knowing I was on track. Gary came and carried the buck the rest of the way back which we figured to be somewhere between half to three quarter miles away.

The landmark that I had to look at was a water tower that was ten miles from where we had parked the pickup.

There were miles of nothing but hills and gullies to look at otherwise. After getting back to the truck I took off my hunting vest. That is when I realized I had no more ammo with me, and my scope was almost falling off my gun from trying to carry my gun and antelope at the same time.

Dad told us to make sure we had enough ammo in case we got separated and were lost to fire two shots in the air, wait a few minutes, and fire two more. Sure, glad I did not get that lost.

The buck was a trophy buck and dressed out seventy-eight pounds of meat. If you figure in the hide, bones, head, gun it was about my total body weight at the time.

Double Fox

To finish the antelope story, on our way back home we saw two fox off in the distance.

We stopped the vehicle and the three of us jumped out Gary and Mark fired before I could get my regular sight lined up as I had removed my scope.

I had a few shells left in the vehicle.

Dust flew up from both of their shots while both fox tried to go down a hole at the same time.

I fired and both foxes dropped.

That one shot was worth $150. The furriers were paying $75 apiece at the time.

Gary and Mark, both patted me on the back and said you deserve it.

That was the one and only time I went Antelope hunting. What an adventure.

I could have gone on and on about hunting stories, but these are some of my favorites.

Pheasant Astronauts

Our back yard in 1965-1966.

In the winter of 1965-1966, there was a huge blizzard that hit our farm. The wind was blowing hard, and snow was piling up in our yard. Looking out our back window to our tree line I saw several pheasants trying to stay out of the wind and snow. There was a globe of ice forming around their heads. It reminded me of the astronauts helmets.

These pheasants were going to suffocate if I did not do something. I dressed up in my warmest clothes, grabbed a fishing landing net and went out in the blinding snow and wind.

This was at the beginning of the storm as it had not hit us hard yet. I captured over 150 pheasants at that time keeping  count of the roasters. I had 75 of them and put them in what we called the brooder house. Small building in our back yard where we raise chicks to chickens in the spring.

I was outside only about a half hour and Mom was not happy with me going out in the storm. When the storm settled, I went out to dig out at least three feet of snow in front of the door and flung open the door and the birds came flying out like crazy. Only one of the rescued birds had died.

Once the snow started melting, we found several other birds that I could not save dead in the snow with a globe of ice on their heads.

Blizzards on the Farm

During this blizzard dad went out in it to get the cows in the barns. He made his way to our milking barn first. Our milk cows were all up close to the milk barn and dad was able to get them in the barn.

Our stock (beef) cows were in a pen next to the milk cow (dairy) pen. That pen had stacks of hay in front of the fence for feeding in the winter and they acted like a wind barrier to protect the cows. The snow was piling up and was going to cover the fence.

Dad needed help.

Dad made his way from the milk barn back to the house and brought with him the lariat rope and a shovel. The snow and wind were picking up.

Mom was so worried as Dad made his way back to the house. It was impossible to see a foot in front for the next step due to blinding snow. Dad knew he had to get our stock cows in the barn, otherwise, the blizzard would kill them.

He tied the lariat rope to himself, Gary, and Mark behind him right away and they headed back out in the storm. Dad led the way and the three of them made it back to the milk barn.

Going through the barn and out the back of the barn. Dad used the back of the barn and fences to guide them to our other barn which we called the red grain barn.

That barn only had grain in two bins on the west side of it with the rest of the barn empty.

They opened the south side doors and were able to drive the stock cows in. They fed the cows with hay and used hay for bedding for them.

Once that was done, the storm got worse. The path back to the house was gone and they needed to make it back. They were able to make their way back by dad leading the way trying to walk straight north into the wind.

Our house was straight north of the milk barn. Making it back to the house they still had to shovel to get the door open to get in.

To get out of the house after this storm Dad had to go out the upstairs window as the snow had entirely buried the door on the main floor of our house.

It was a good thing that he had brought the shovel into the house earlier. Dad started shoveling until he could get down to the front porch. Once he was able to get the front door open Gary and Mark helped with shoveling the snow, making a path all the way to the milk barn which was around 100 yards from the house.

I know it took several hours to get there. I don't think we lost any livestock due to dads quick actions.

The cars and tractors were completely covered with snow. Wayne and I worked digging them out. Well, I should say we helped dig them out.

I remember that Susan, Gary, Mark, Wayne, and I all had to walk three-quarters of a mile to get on the school bus when school opened for a few days. Yes, both ways and it was not a joke.

There were two more bad blizzards that hit our farm that I can remember. However, I had already left the farm and we had much better equipment to plow out. Winters of 1976/77 and 1996/97. After that third blizzard mom decided to move to town in a lull between Christmas and New Years. She did not get back to the farm until April.

Pearl and Pal

We raised cattle, some we milked, and the rest were stock (beef) cows. Dad bought us a couple of ponies. One

little black and white Shetland stallion and one Welsh female pony who was much bigger. We named the stallion Pal and the Welsh pony we named Pearl. (Photo: Susan with Pal and Pearl.)

These ponies helped us with cattle drives and daily use for sorting out the milk cows from stock cows in the pasture.

Pal was a nice-looking little pony but had the temperament of a large stallion being mean and stubborn.

Pal would buck and try to bite you if you didn't pay close attention to him. He was a lot harder to break for us kids to ride then I think anyone expected.

Dad broke him by sitting on him. Dads feet were on the ground while straddling Pal. When Pal tried to buck dad off, dad would raise his feet off the ground. The little pony couldn't buck with a 6'1-inch man weighing approximately

240 pounds at the time. The little pony Pal would finally calm down. Dad would put one of us kids on Pal and then lead him around until dad trusted him enough to let us ride him.

All of us that rode Pal were bitten, bucked off, rubbed up against a barb wire fence or rolled off in the creek.

That little pony never ever really gave into us and was always looking for a way to get rid of us, but he was still our Pal which we rode daily.

Pearl was easier to break for riding and generally a good pony for us but she was quite a bit bigger than Pal.

I mostly had ridden Pal as he was much easier to get on. Wayne rode Pearl, being older than me he always got his choice of ride.

We all rode Pal bareback. Our only saddle was too big for him.

I could grab onto Pal's mane and hop up on his back; whereas Pearl I would have to lead her over to the stock yard wood fence and climb on the fence and hop on her back.

Pal and Barbed Wire

The summer of 1969, when I was eleven years old, was one of the most memorable years of my youth.

One of mine and Waynes daily chores was to take our ponies out to the pasture to get the milk cows and bring them back to the stock yard.

Wayne would ride Pearl and I rode Pal.

That summer Wayne was spending time at Grandma and Grandpa Bergs house, helping them out.

Grandma was not feeling well and Wayne, being 13 years old, was a big help to them.

One day while riding Pal he decided he didn't want me to be on him and he rubbed me up against the barb wire fence putting two deep gashes on my right leg just below the knee from the barb wire.

Mom patched me up with Mercurochrome (reddish orange disinfectant) and band aids. I think I should have had stitches as to this day I still have scars from that incident.

Pal and Creek Rollover

A few days later Pal tried to buck me off and couldn't; so he then ran to the creek bed and rolled over to get me off.

He did roll me off, but I held onto the reins and hopped back on him.

Like every day, we brought milk cows to the barn to milk. That day, I and Pal were both full of mud from head to toe.

Thinking back, I think both incidents happened because Wayne and Pearl were not with us. Pal didn't like it.

After both of those incidents, I decided that I could ride Pearl.

(In this 1975 photo I am holding Farrah, named by Wayne after Farrah Fawcett-- his favorite poster-girl at that time. Farrah was the colt of Raytez, our quarter horse.)

Pearl-Gate

One day both Mom and Dad were working out in the field. My older brothers Gary and Mark were milking cows. Neal was playing near the house and Susan was doing laundry hanging towels on the clothesline.

Dad had made a small walk-through gate on the west side of the barn. It was a homemade pipe gate that dad had welded together. On the side of the gate there were three pieces of pipe welded to use as hinges. Dad made hinge bolts hangers that the gate was hung on. These bolts had a washer and nut with approximately two to three inches of thread sticking out the back side of the post.

That little gate was very handy as it was the access point to the stock yard without having to climb the fence or go through the barn to access the stock yard. It was just big enough to lead the ponies through, which I had done a few times with both Pal and Pearl.

The gate was not wide enough to ride the ponies through, however.

I led Pearl through the barn that morning and took her out riding to the field where Mom was working, Then, I rode her back home.

I hadn't noticed that the little side gate that dad had recently installed on the west side of the barn was open. After riding around our front yard for a little while, Pearl noticed the gate was open and started galloping toward it.

I knew that I and the pony would never fit through that little gate and pulled back hard on the reins. This caused Pearl to rare up and throw me off before she ran through the gate leaving me behind.

When I flew off her back my head hit the top bolt with the threads sticking out.

I was stunned and when I stood up, I could feel something warm running down my face. I looked over to the side of the barn and saw a streak of blood squirting on it with every heartbeat blood would spurt out.

I started to scream and luckily my sister Susan was outside and heard me and came to my aid. I don't remember much of how and who drove me to the hospital.

(Email from my brother Gary,)

I was visiting with Susan last week and she mentioned you had called her checking details about your accident falling off Pearl. Here is what I remember:

Mark and I were milking when we heard your screaming in the middle of the yard. When we looked out the barn door, your head was full of blood. Maybe Mark can clarify, but I think he ran out to get Mom in the field north of the farm and I believe Dad was in the small field south of the pasture.

I think you were able to walk to the house. Maybe Susan cleaned up some of your blood.

Anyway, our folks came home as quickly as they could and took you to Dr. Bloemendaal at the Ipswich Hospital where he cleared out all the hair and broken bone tissue.

Apparently, (based on comments from Mom and Dad) doctors even then were supposed to have two doctors present when working on brains.

Once Dr. Bloemendaal got you cleaned up, he had Mom and Dad came into the emergency room with you. According to Dad, Dr. Bloemendaal described what he did-- cut your hair on the side of your head, pulled out bone fragments, and cleaned up blood.

Then he said, "I have no idea what kind of brain damage occurred. It may not be apparent right away--maybe long-term damage since you were quite young."

Dr. Bloemendaal covered the side of your head with bandage. Either he had or ordered a plastic skull protector. [It looked like a thick piece of hard plastic about four inches wide with a softer (cloth) wrapping on top and bottom to keep the protective plastic from touching your head. It was in a semicircle that wrapped around from one side (eyebrow) of your head, around the back, to the other side (eyebrow).]

He said you had to wear that all the time. (I think for a year until the skin and cartilage grew over the bolt hole.) Dr. Bloemendaal also said, head bones do not regrow, so you will always be missing that bone that he removed.

You were absolutely prohibited from playing sports or reckless play.

When Mom and Dad came home, a couple hours later, we ate supper late and they told us about you and the operation. I distinctly remember Dad, with tasteless humor, saying, "Well I know at least one of you has brains. I saw Wesley's."

Since he has a very good memory (but not as good as Mom's), Wayne maybe can give more details, too. But I really think you need to talk to Mark also to get details of what he remembers.

You have no idea how many times people prayed for your recovery. God has certainly looked after you all these years....Gary

(Email from Mark,)

HI All,

Wes after reading Gary's account of "Pearl-Gate" I really don't have anything to add. His description is probably quite accurate, certainly detailed.

I do know I was close by when it happened and remember you scaring the heck out of us with your bloody head. Then Mom and Dad took you to see Dr. Bloemendaal.

I do still have clear visual of that top gate bolt with your hair on it--frightening!

I can't relate anything to the incident that would help pin down the date it happened.

Knowing you, you probably backed Pearl up against the far south corral fence near the water tank and tried to see how fast you and her could go through the gate…just speculation.

It's neat you are trying to capture your adventures.

Gary thanks for the details and pulling out some family pictures.

Us siblings certainly have been blessed with angels watching over us through the years!....Mark

(Email from Neal,)

I recall that I was playing in front of the house that day. Wes was riding Pearl I think coming back from riding to the field and she ran and stopped at the gate and Wes was thrown off and hit his head on the gate bolt.

I recall hearing him screaming and then seeing him walking by the barn with blood coming out each time his heart beat.

I do not recall much after that, but what has been stated seems correct.

I think, Wes, you started to wrestle fairly soon after the incident. Didn't you make varsity in Jr high?

I recall you passing out while wrestling at Northwestern when you were a senior. I sat with you in the locker room after you recovered.

Yes, as a family, God has taken care of all of us and our families.

Love you all! Neal

This is what I recall:

I do remember being in the hospital operating room with Doctor Bloemendaal and his nurse (Mrs. Omland) working on me. There was a white cloth draped across my face feeling something moving around in my head.

I could hear the doctor and nurse talking and removing broken pieces of bone from my head scraping and crunching sounds. I heard the doctor say to me you need to stay awake.

My dad and mom were in the operating room the whole time talking to me to keep me awake. I needed to stay awake so the doctor could tell how well he and the nurse were doing removing the broken pieces.

I was able to stay awake the whole time as it took several hours. I think it was eight hours with the cloth draped across my face.

I do recall dad telling me that he knew I was a smart kid because he could see that I had brains which made me smile.

After the surgery, I was taken to a bedroom, and I remember asking mom if I had to stay there because the room smelled funny. She laughed and said yes, I had to stay, and I should get some sleep.

I don't think it took more than a second for me to fall asleep.

The next morning, I remember waking up with mom in the room. She asked how I was feeling? I think I said my head hurt.

She then got up and told the nurse that I was awake. The doctor was in the room quickly. He put a light in my eyes, told nurse Omland to give me some pills, and then asked mom and dad to see him in the hallway.

I could hear them talking. I heard the Doctor tell mom and dad that he thought that I would recover, and they need to keep a close eye on me. Also, I would have to stay in the hospital for a few days.

He then told them that I may not be able to walk because I may have lost my ability to balance due to the injury being very close to my medulla obligati. It will be a wait and see situation.

That really scared me.

What the heck is medulla obligati anyway ran through my head. (Actually, it is called the medulla oblongata.)

He also told them that I would need a helmet.

I thought I must have dreamt that because the pills made me tired. I fell back to sleep.

When I woke up again Dr. Bloemendaal told nurse Omland that she should get me anything that I wanted to eat. The only thing that she mentioned that I wanted was ice cream and orange soda. She made me an orange float.

I think I asked for an orange float every day I was in the hospital, and they gave it to me. I was very happy.

I tried getting out of bed and setting off some alarms. Nurse Omland came into the room right away, turned off the alarms and asked me what I was doing. I told her I had to go to the bathroom, and I didn't want to go in a pan again. She said we will try and helped me to my feet.

She was surprised I was able to walk without much help. Dr. Bloemendaal came to the room shortly after and told nurse Omland to take me for a walk in the hall. The doctor was amazed and put me on a walking schedule.

He knew I liked soda and told nurse Omland to give me a key for the soda machine so I could get one whenever I wanted one.

Being in a small-town hospital I'm sure I was the first and last one to ever have that privilege. It was a way for the doctor to see my progression in walking as the pop machine was in the hall several feet from my room and I had to pass the nurse station to get to it.

After a few days of being in the hospital I was able to go home. I was not sure I really wanted to as I was treated extremely well at the hospital, and I knew I would not get soda or orange floats whenever I wanted one at home.

A few weeks after I was home. Mom let me go outside. I really needed to prove to myself I still had my balance and walked the board fence that nearly killed me a few weeks earlier.

The extra threads were sawed off and smoothed out on that gate post when I got home.

Wrestling

As Gary mentioned in his email, I had to wear a helmet and was restricted from any sports. That was tough for me. My entire seventh grade I had to watch other kids playing baseball, football, basketball, and wrestling while being teased about the helmet.

I did get to do cross country running, which I really did not like but at least I got to do something related to a sport that year.

I had to wear that helmet for nearly that entire year until I put up such a fit telling mom no more. That was the only thing that worked with mom at the time.

In Neal's email he mentioned that I was in wrestling. In the eighth grade I was able to get mom and dad to let me go out for wrestling only a year after my head injury.

All my brothers were participating in wrestling. Neal and even Kent were in AAU kid wrestling programs. Wayne, Mark, and Gary were all on Ipswich high school varsity teams.

I made the high school varsity team also by beating out two sophomores at 119 lb. weight class. As an eighth grader, I lettered that year.

One night we had a match with Faulkton--one of the top teams in the state the year prior. I almost pinned the previous year's state champion in the second period of my match.

I did end up losing that match by points, but it was a big deal, I had my picture in the Newspaper.

Mark was the only one on the team that won a match that night. I always had to try to not get tied up in headlocks, so I had to be quick at leg takedowns.

Throughout my high school wrestling I was on the varsity team in different weight classes.

I recall getting knocked out once and passing out twice through those years on the team.

I set a school record for having the fastest pin of five seconds.

The bad thing was the record was broken the year after I graduated from high school. I believe that record still stands today at a three-second pin.

Track and Field

The only other sport I was allowed to do was track and field.

I did high jump, shot put, discus and ran the 880 on the medley relay team. I tried pole vaulting until one day at attempting an eleven foot vault at practice. I went way over the bar and missed the mats entirely landing on my back. Knocking the wind out of me and giving me a headache.

Coach pulled me out of the pole-vaulting event.

I was a sophomore in high school at a track meet in Mobridge, South Dakota. I had finished my events and went to the bus to eat my lunch. Two of my teammates were already on the bus doing the same thing.

It was a warm day, and my teammates opened all the windows on the bus to let the air flow through. By the time I came the bus, it had cooled down some from having the windows open. It felt good in there.

I started to eat my sandwich and a few kids from the town of Mobridge started throwing water balloons at the bus's with open windows thinking they were cool.

We knew they were not track and field kids as they were dressed in street clothes and smoking cigarettes. The three of us started closing the windows so we would not have the bus full of water balloons.

As I was closing a window a balloon was coming my way. I caught the balloon and heaved it right back to the kid that threw it. The balloon hit him right in the face.

He happened to have his cigarette in his mouth, and he swallowed it.

That really started a war. These boys were mad and tried to get onto the bus. Mike, one of my teammates, held the back door shut and Tim, my other teammate, was holding the handle to the front doors. I continued to try closing the windows.

By this time the kids outside were trying to get in through the windows. The bus had windows on both sides, and I could not close them all.

Tim and Mike decided to run to get some help. They both bolted out the front of the bus when the group outside concentrated on the windows. This left both doors unprotected with me right in the middle of the bus.

Those kids came at me from both sides.

Mobridge is a cowboy town, and all these kids were wearing cowboy boots. I was getting a real beating with two of the guys kicking me and at least one punching me.

Luckily, Tim and Mike came back with half the track team and our coach. All the kids that attacked me bolted out the back door of the bus with our track team after them.

Coach jumped in the driver's seat and took after the bunch. He yelled at our team boys to stop and get on the bus. He then pursued the attackers with the bus.

They ran several blocks and went into a gas station. Coach made everyone stay on the bus and he went in. I don't know what they told him, but I ended up being the bad guy.

Tim and Mike defended me with the coach. Coach drove us back to the track field and picked up the rest of the team. The track meet had ended and everyone that was not already on the bus got on.

Our team trainer came to me and was cleaning me up as I had blood and cuts all over my body. I looked like I was in a heavy weight fight with Mohammad Ali (the greatest prize fighter of that time).

Coach asked me if I had to go to the hospital. I refused, saying if I needed the hospital it could wait until we were back in Ipswich.

I forgot to mention our bus driver had left the bus to get a drink and something to eat at the concession stand when all this happened. He was first worried that the bus had been stolen.

Coach sat next to me all the way back to Ipswich asking me questions. I thought for sure I was going to be kicked off the team.

Dad picked me up from school after we had gotten back, he talked a little bit to our coach. We drove home without hardly saying a word.

I could tell dad was mad and when dad gets mad which he rarely did, you are better off just staying quiet.

Dad gave me quite the speech when we got home. I don't know what the coach told dad, but I was sure he didn't give dad the full story.

Dad stayed mad at me until he heard the story in town the next day. Dad then felt really bad as he had been sure it was my fault.

It took me about a month before the black and blue marks were nearly gone. I did not get kicked off the team, but my high jumping and other events suffered for a while till I healed up.

Rattled at Grandparents

As I mentioned earlier Wayne stayed with Grandma and Grandpa Berg helping them. He had to come home for something--I'm not sure why, but I got to stay with our maternal grandparents for a week.

During that week I helped Grandpa with the dairy cows and mowed the yard.

One thing that we were taught by mom was to always be on the lookout for rattle snakes on Grandpas farm.

One afternoon I was going to the stock yard to get the cows in the barn for milking. The cows would not go in the barn.

I did not understand why until I started walking up to the barn door and heard that distinct rattle. There was a huge rattlesnake right in front of the barn door. It was the first rattlesnake I had ever seen in person.

I ran as hard as I could to the house to get Grandpa. He grabbed a pitchfork and killed the snake. It had eight rattles on it. Grandpa was so proud of me for not getting too close and getting him.

Two days later I was to mow their lawn. While mowing a snake stuck its head up behind the mower. I quickly pulled the mower back over it and left the mower running.

I once again took off for the house. Grandpa came out with a 22-rifle and looked for the snake but it was nowhere to be found.

I was so afraid that it took me a long time to finish mowing as I went very slow making sure if there was a snake the mower would get it.

Sows

When age appropriate, pigs were second in line of progression for outside chores.

We raised pigs both open range as it is called these days and pen raised.

The open range pigs were fed and watered in troughs that my dad had made using old water heater tanks cut in half with stabilizer bars welded to the bottoms to keep the hogs from dumping out the water, milk, and grains we fed them.

We fed and raised these pigs in the hog pasture which was mainly a ten acre alfalfa field.

Once a sow was pregnant, we would sort her out and move her to a barn with furrowing pens in it. Sows were allowed to roam in and out to the hog barn until it was time to have piglets. Then, each sow was put in a furrowing pen for her piglet's protection.

Sow hogs can and do get very mean before and especially after piglets are born. One always had to be on alert to the changing habits of a sow as they could easily tear you to pieces without a care on their part.

My brothers and I luckily were able to outrun the pigs and were able to get away from these vicious attacks. This is the other reason for furrowing pens.

I know animal right activist do not like the idea of furrowing pens, but I know what these hogs can do to a person.

Furrowing pens are bolted down to a cement floor and are made of one-inch square tubing. We had some sows rip the bolts right out of the concrete floor or bend the steel tubing up with their heads. Tremendous amount of strength these animals have.

Sows can have upwards of twenty or more piglets; most of ours had between eight and eighteen when they gave birth.

Sows that are free range hogs when giving birth, many of their piglets die within the first couple of days from being trampled or laid on by their mother.

Dead ones are often eaten by their mothers or other hogs near them.

Furrowing pens reduce the death rate but sadly there are still piglets that do not make it.

I do have to say that a piglet is one of the cutest little animals when young.

One time there was a sow that Wayne and I could not get moved to the barn before she had her litter. That summer Wanye had gotten a job to work at the school in town and was not available to help me with the task to come.

The sow had a litter of eighteen piglets that had to be removed from the hog pasture to the barn. Otherwise, we likely would have lost all the piglets due to several other hogs, including a big boar, in the hog pasture. Chances for survival was very slim had we left them in the pasture with adult hogs.

The hogs nest was made in a pile of hay about twenty yards from the fence line. This was an older sow--very big and very mean.

She just finished having the litter, so they were small newborn piglets. Trying to move her was going to be a problem.

I went and set up a cardboard box that I lined with straw on the outside of the pasture fence. I dumped grain in the feeder to get the sow away from her piglets.

Then I climbed over the fence and would grab as many piglets as I could. I quickly ran over to the fence and put them in the box. It worked for two trips, and I was able to get twelve piglets in the box.

By that time the sow was aware of what I was doing and on my last trip I grabbed the remaining six piglets. I knew I had to do something different this time as the sow was on my trail.

I ran as hard as I could with piglets in tow and jumped to get over the fence. She caught my pant leg and ripped a piece of my blue jeans off as I fell over the fence.

I rolled with the piglets in my arms a few times, got up and ran all the way to the hog barn before stopping. I was not sure if the fence was going to hold that sow back.

I went back to collect the box of remaining piglets. I put them with a sow that had only six piglets and waited till I had help to get the sow from the pasture as I did not want to take another chance by myself with her.

Shocked Porkers

Another one of my experiences that could have been disastrous for me was while feeding pigs. We had a big round hog feeder in the hog pen.

We would fill the feeder with ground up grain mixture using an electric auger. The auger would be placed on the top of the hog feeder and run over a fence with the end of the auger buried into the grain inside of our metal grain wagon.

We would get that auger all set up and stand in the grain to feed the end of the auger with grain using an aluminum scoop shovel with a wooden handle. Once it was all setup we would plug in the auger.

It had rained the night before I was to fill the hog feeder and the ground was wet and muddy. The feeder was nearly empty, so the hogs were very excited to see that I was going to fill the feeder.

The second I plugged in the electric auger, I felt a jolt run through my body, heard the pigs squeal--a terrible squeal, and I jumped out of the grain wagon. I still had the electric cord in my hand, and it unplugged as I flew out of the wagon.

I looked over at the hog feeder and saw a terrible sight of eight of our prize hogs lying dead in a perfect circle around the feeder.

I had the feeling that I was next to be dead once my folks found out what I had done.

I'm sure I let out a scream myself as my brother was upon me in a flash with my mother not far behind.

Scared to death--what would my father do when he heard of this accident.

My mother and I jumped in our pickup truck and drove out to the field where my father was working. He did not say much of anything, just hopped in the truck behind the wheel and drove out of the field like a tornado was chasing us down.

We pulled the pigs out of the pen and drove directly to the meat locker in town to have the hogs processed. We ended up buying a new freezer to store all the pork we had. None of the meat was lost due to my father's quick action.

To my surprise I was not scolded or punished for this happening. I was just told to put a new cord on the auger.

We had plenty of good protein for the family for the entire year from a one second occurrence.

(L-R) Mark, Mom, and I am next to hay dump rake (left) with hog feeder in background.

Calf Tale

On the farm, cattle often break through areas of barb wire fencing and get out into fields that they should not be in.

When I was very young, a calf was on the wrong side of the fence. I wanted to show my family that I could round up this calf and get it back where it belonged.

The pursuit began and the calf tried to make a fool out of me running the opposite direction I wanted it to go.

I ran after him as he crossed the road a quarter mile from our house and he continued to run further east.

First off, I had never been past our driveway before on my own and was a little concerned that I would get scolded for leaving the farmstead.

I tried many times to get around that calf running twice as far and get it to turn back toward home without success. By that time the calf ran another mile east to Highway 45 and shot across the road. Luckily, there was no traffic.

The calf was getting tired by that time and laid down. I was also exhausted.

I really did not want to spook him anymore and made a wide long loop around him, so I was facing his backside slowly snuck up on him and pounced on him. I had him and sat with him for a while to catch my breath. Making sure he calmed down and giving both of us some much-needed rest.

Now that I had him, how was I going to get him back home?

I took my belt off and put it around the calve's neck to hold on to him. My belt barely went around his neck so that would not work.

I walked him back to the highway and I tried to pick him up by reaching around all four legs like I saw my dad and older brothers do. He was much too heavy for me. I was able to walk him across the Highway holding onto his neck.

I sat down again and rested a little bit more once across the highway when I saw our pickup with dust flying behind coming toward me and the calf.

Relieved, I held onto the calf as he was trying to get away again and I could not let that happen.

At that point I was feeling so proud of myself for catching that calf. Extremely happy that I would not have to try walking the calf all the way back home.

The truck pulled up and my dad was behind the wheel. Dad looked at the calf and me both sweating from the pursuit and to my surprise he was not very happy.

He picked the calf up, tied its legs together so it could not jump out of the back of the pickup and then looked at me very angry.

He then threw a rope around me saying if you are going to act like a dog, I'm going to treat you like a dog.

My pride turned to very scared and I started to cry.

Dad took the rope off me, tossed me in on the passenger side of the truck and headed for home. Not another word was said until the calf was back with its mother.

Dad then said to me, "what were you thinking" that was a long way from home for you and the calf. Both you and the calf could have been seriously hurt.

I knew that I was not going to be able to explain why and felt it was best just to sit and listen. I don't know if I ever really got over that experience, but when I was a child, I was extremely afraid of my dad for a long time after that.

After I had children of my own, I realized that the experience that took place with my dad and the calf had more to do with extreme worry for me than the calf.

The long hours of hard work that my father had to do to support our family caused his reaction toward me at that moment. Dad was a very loving and caring father.

Readers, please understand my dad was a very good kind man that had the pressures of feeding seven kids while caring for his father that lived with us. He managed the farm and worked eight-hour days as a mechanic in town.

Mom also worked as a cook in town. My parents tried to work in shifts in my early years, putting sixteen to eighteen hours a day at times between town jobs and farm jobs. That would be enough to break anyone down emotionally from time to time.

Nailed by Dad

After several years of working as a mechanic, Dad took a new job working for the Ipswich Lumber Company. One of the funnier stories about dad happened there. Dad could work with anybody and was an extremely hard worker.

One summer a hailstorm went through the area and the lumber yard had a lot of homes to replace and shingle roofs.

One of Mark's senior high school classmates, Darwin, worked at the lumber yard with dad. Darwin's dad also worked at the lumber yard and their family attended church services with us.

Darwin told us the story at a mission festival dinner. He said dad was so fast at nailing shingles down with the hammer and nail. Darwin was to lay the shingle in place and dad then came along and nailed them in place.

Darwin said he was laying the shingles down and he was not fast enough for dad. Most of the time, it only took dad one hit of the hammer on the nail and it was in solid. Other guys pounded at least three or more times.

Darwin said one time he was really moving along laying the shingles. He thought he was quite aways ahead of dad. When a nail went through the tip of his glove dad had caught up with him and accidentally nailed his glove to the roof. Darwin said he had to get to be faster at his job after that.

Dad Could Do Anything

My father was a master of many trades. Dad could solve any problem that came up on the farm from fixing broken equipment to caring for animals, plumbing, electrical work, and much more. We never took anything to anybody to have it worked on. Everything was handled right on the farm.

One time the rear end gear box on the tractor needed to be replaced.

I remember dad coming home from his job at six p.m., having dinner with us, and then going out to the tractor. He tore the whole back end of the tractor apart.

I helped get him the tools he needed. I was to break down cardboard boxes that came with cases of cereal that mom bought at Prairie Market. The cardboard was laid on the ground so the tractor parts could be sorted and kept clean.

This included the rear axle and all. I could not believe how many little parts there were. Dad replaced everything that night--finishing up around three a.m.

He then went to bed for about two hours getting up at five a.m. putting together the projects for the field work that needed to be done for the day. He had a bite to eat before heading out to his job at the lumber yard at six a.m.

Many times, during the harvest time, he would be out in the fields till midnight if conditions were applicable to do so.

Mom the Farmer

I told you a little bit about mom training us to do house chores. Mom never really liked house chores herself. She would much rather be out in the field on the tractor than cleaning the house.

Mom did a lot of field work from plowing, to mowing hay, and raking it. This is one of the reasons my sister Susan never got away from housework.

Mom washed clothes regularly until Susan was old enough to take over. Susan also took care of us, doing the babysitting so to speak. This freed mom to do more outside the house.

If mom was not out in the field, she would be found in the garden working. Don't get me wrong, mom was an extremely hard worker. She just didn't like to do it in the house. She did enjoy cooking and canning. Mom was an excellent cook.

When we slaughtered a cow, pig, or processed deer Mom liked to help out with it. Mom was excellent at making sausage. She was our quality control agent for packaging and making sure everything was sanitized during the process.

I learned a lot from mom working with her while processing meat. I think that is why I took to meat cutting and managing meat departments as a career.

Mom was also the money manager in the family. Dad and mom did budgets and planning together but mom controlled the purse strings.

She was not going to be treated the way my grandfather treated our grandmother--only getting enough money to get by with. Mom would sell our extra cream and eggs where she could. Because she spoke German, she made deals with the Hutterites exchanging cream for other food commodities.

The Cream Lady

The Hutterites one day ordered cream from mom who they called "The Cream Lady." Our dog followed her to Pembrook Colony. They had been our neighbor since 1970.

Mom was visiting with the Colony manager when our dog came into their driveway. Out the passenger side-window mom heard the Hutterite boys say in German. Get the gun to shoot that dog. Mom scolded them in German "You will not shoot my dog." It shocked them. They didn't know the "Cream Lady" could speak German.

(Note: Hutterites are farm-oriented Anabaptists who use modern technology and equipment but operate as communal colonies. They are pacifists and only use guns to control predators, like dogs that sometimes formed roaming packs and killed calves at night. Often called Hutterian Brethren, they are mainly concentrated in sixty-two South Dakota colonies--currently about ten percent of the state's farmers.)

Tractors

We had an International-H tractor and a couple years later we added a Minneapolis Moline tractor with a hand clutch. Both tractors had side-by-side (narrow) front wheels.

When out working in the fields hitting badger holes in summer or frozen cow pies in winter the front end made the ride very interesting.

The tractor would be kind of like a horse--it would buck the front of the tractor upwards breaking parts on the tractor or attached equipment. Not to mention occasional rock getting stuck between the wheels requiring a metal rod to pry the rock out.

Dad changed the front end of the H tactor first on the farm in the front yard. Having the front wheel axel changed spreading the wheels apart. This allowed the tractor to ride much smoother, better for front end loader operations and field work. He later did the same with the Minneapolis Moline.

Dad did all the mechanical work on our farm. As I entered my teenage years dad had purchased a model 756-International tractor with a cab and radio in it. That was a really big deal for us!

Our three tractors are packing our silage pile next to hay bales.

Haying

Haying was a summer job that required a lot of physical labor and many hours out in the fields all summer long. Haying required many more hours than what was needed with grain and corn crops.

Mom, or one of my older brothers, would mow prairie grasses and alfalfa fields with the H-International using a side sickle mower. An old, originally horse-drawn dump rake was attached to the mower behind the tractor.

One of us kids would be tied, across our lap with a rope or old belt, to the seat on the dump rake. Dump raking was one of our very first jobs working in the fields.

The dump rake used a foot dumping mechanism for lifting the tines of the rake and dumping the hay that was raked up in windrows. It was a chore that I think most of us liked to do even though our butts were quite sore after a few hours of riding on that metal seat.

The rake did not have any sort of shock absorbers, just two big iron wheels that traveled across the bumpy mounds of gopher and badger holes. Likewise, glaciated rocks, that were small enough to leave in the field, felt like boulders when riding that rake.

Raking taught us timing skills in a way that I don't think could have been taught better any other way. Timing was required in many ways.

First we needed to figure out how big of a windrow would be acceptable for the baler that came after raking was finished. The hay had to have time to dry out for baling.

Then timing was required for every time after to get the dumps so that you could make straight rows as you continued across the fields.

Timing was challenging. Every few seconds I had to anticipate the next dump, regardless, if I hit a badger hole making the rake bounce, and so would I.

Raking was one of my favorite times as I got to spend time with my mother for hours. We would take breaks together. Water, oranges, or apples never tasted better than they did when we were cutting and raking hay. We even chewed on the orange peeling while haying just to keep our mouths moist.

One summer I jumped off the dump rake and landed directly in a badger hole with my right foot going down the hole, and badly twisting my ankle. I had to walk using crutches for six weeks in the beginning of the haying season.

My two oldest brothers, Gary and Mark, were bailing and working in other fields. Susan was our cook, house cleaner, and babysitter of Kent and Neal. I believe Wayne was staying with Grandma and Grandpa Berg for a few weeks to help them out.

This left an opening for a dump rake rider which my younger brother, Neal, promoted to be the dump rake rider. Neal was much smaller than me and could not have been much older than seven or eight years old.

While sitting on the seat of the dump rake, Neal could not kick down on the foot dumping mechanism. The rake also had a lever dumping mechanism that could be pushed forward to dump the hay.

Mom, being creative, belted Neal to the seat so he would not fall off. She then tied a rope to the handle of the dump rake to assist Neal with the dumping. This served two purposes: one, mom would know where Neal was all the time, and secondly, it worked as a teaching lesson.

Mom worked with Neal for about three or four days before deciding that I could handle driving the tractor with

Neal on the rake. Having a sprained ankle did not keep me from my haying duties. My ankle being badly sprained gave me a promotion so to speak.

We had to switch tractors used to mow. I am three years older than Neal and was promoted to be the driver and mower operator.

The Minneapolis Moline tractor had a hand clutch for shifting gears so I would not have to use the foot clutch. With me hobbling on crutches and Neal looking so small tied down to the seat on the dump rake, that had to be quite the sight.

Neal and my first dumps and windrows were not the best. Timing took a while for us to get used to it. Neal pushed down as hard as he could while I was mowing, driving, and pulling hard enough on the rope to get the rake to dump. We quickly learned.

That summer, Neal, with his always happy smile and quick wit for a little kid, allowed the two-or-three-weeks to go by quickly with Wayne gone.

Baling

After mowing and raking, hay baling was the next stage. We had a New Holland rectangle bailer that was pulled behind the H tractor or 756 International. Then, behind the baler we had a skid.

The homemade skid was made up of two-by-ten-inch plank boards that had a space in the middle of the skid to drop the end of a pry bar into the ground. The bar was used to slide a stack of bales off the skid. The skid was attached to the baler with a log chain hooked to the hitch of the baler.

The pry bar was one inch in diameter steel rod. When not being used, it was held in a pipe that had a flat piece of metal welded to it which was bolted onto the skid.

The person riding the skid would catch the bales as they came out of the baler and stack six bales on the skid. Three bales were placed on their sides so that the ground would not rot the twine holding them together. On top of those, two more bales were laid perpendicular across the lower three, and one more bale was on top.

Once the stack of six bales was done, the stacking person would take the metal bar and jab it into dirt between the slot on the skid and let the forward movement of the tractor and bailer work to slide the bales off the skid onto the ground.

Here again timing was needed as the bales slid off the skid. There were more bales coming out of the baler. Hay bales weigh somewhere between sixty to eighty pounds each depending on the type of hay. Sometimes, the alfalfa bales' weight ranged from eighty to a hundred-and-twenty pounds each depending on the quality, moisture content, and length of the bale.

Baling made us boys strong.

Lightening

One time my older brother Gary and I were out baling straw. Gary was in the 756 International tractor driving and I was on the bale skid stacking bales. We were down to our last couple windrows of rye straw in the field when the wind started to pick up.

We could see a storm coming in from the west a few miles away. The sky above us only had some scattered clouds. We both thought it was great. We would be able to finish this field and get home before the rain hits.

We made it three quarters through the second to last windrow when a bolt of lightning struck. Gary stated that the lightning hit in front of the tractor and he saw dust or smoke lift straight up where it hit, which I'm sure it did.

I know that lightning bolts split while one part hit in front of the tractor, and the other part hit the steal push rod on the skid.

No more than a second earlier I had just placed the rod in the holder and removed my hand from the rod when the lightning struck.

I was thrown from the skid ten-to-fifteen feet away and had a hole burnt through the sole of my shoe from that lighting strike.

I could feel every bit of my body tingle and it took me a few seconds to figure out what had happened.

I think having leather gloves on my hands and not having a hand on the push bar saved my life. This definitely could have turned out much worse for both of us.

Once we gathered our wits about us, we quickly headed for home which was about three-quarters of a mile away. We had to wait a couple of days for the windrows to dry out before finishing that little bit that was left.

Hauling and Stacking Bales

Bales were not left in the field for very long once baling was completed. It was time to load the bales on a hay wagon and this required at least two people. It was always better when we had three people: one person on the tractor, one on the hay wagon for stacking bales, and one on the ground to toss the bales on the wagon.

We went from small stack to small stack in the field picking up the stacks of six bales. We would trade off positions from ground to wagon regularly to try to be fair to each other.

I really do not think that made much of a difference as stacking them on the wagon was just as hard if not harder sometimes then walking between stacks and then throwing them up to the wagon.

I don't recall how many bales were stacked on the wagon—maybe ninety to a hundred.

Once the wagon was full, we needed to haul them back to the farmstead where we then had to hand unload the wagon stacking the bales once again into large stacks. Every muscle in your body ached for days until the job was done.

Remember, regular daily chores had to be done besides the hauling bales.

Upgrades Needed

Mom and dad knew that baling of hay (the way we were doing it) would have to end as the family was getting smaller.

Dad investigated big round balers and decided that it would be too costly for us. He would not only have to buy the bigger baler, but he would also have to upgrade all of our other equipment to move those thousand-pound bales.

Dad and mom decided on buying a new hay stacking piece of equipment instead. I was then a nineth grader. This hay stacker was called a Haybuster.

The Haybuster worked somewhat like the baler, but it was a large piece of equipment that needed to be pulled by a larger tractor. This is when the 756 International tractor was put to work more.

The Haybuster could hold up to at least 10,000 lbs. or more of hay. This Haybuster had a large round flatbed sixteen feet in diameter. A metal cage was around it to hold the hay as it was being picked up.

Hay was pushed up a long chute that was equipped with a hydraulic arm on top. That arm was moved by the tractor driver using hydraulic levers. The arm would be moved from side to side and up and down to stack and pack the hay as it entered a large round cage.

Once the Haybuster stack was completed, the tractor driver would either take the entire stack back to the farmstead, if the hay was within a mile of home, or the stack was unloaded close to a road for moving later.

The entire stack was unloaded by lifting the shaft arm to its highest point. (Just guessing at this point), it had to be nearly thirty feet in the air.

The cage had two large swing gates to the back of the stacker that could only be opened by hand. This meant that the driver needed to climb out of the tractor, open the Haybuster gates, climb back into the tractor, back the stacker in position, and work levers for unloading.

With the hydraulics, the bed of the Haybuster would tilt the bed of the stack until the back end almost touched the ground. This was one of the slowest processes as you did not want the stack to tip out and fall over.

There were two heavy duty chains with raised grips under the stack of hay that would roll the stack of hay off the stacker to the ground. These chains were also part of the hydraulic system that the driver would work another lever slowly and drive the tractor forward at the same time to unload the haystack.

The first haystack was always the hardest to unload as it would be unloaded freestanding--with no support. The first one was the first link for the many more haystacks to follow.

We would have many haystacks in a row. When we were done placing the haystacks in a row. They would look like a row of hills from a distance.

Dad and Wayne did just about all the stacking the first year. Gary and Mark were in the Air Force.

While this stacker was much more efficient and less labor intense, that didn't mean it did not have its problems. Regularly, we wore out bearing's that pushed the hay up through the chute.

The photo above shows dad sitting on the ground working on replacing bearings. Mom is standing in front of him. The main reason was the only bearings that were available for this piece of equipment had been under water from a flood that hit the plant where they were made.

Dad, Wayne, and I got pretty good at tearing down the front end of the stacker replacing bearings and putting it back together.

I started stacking hay my sophomore year in high school with this stacker. My junior and senior years I did almost all of the hay stacking. Dad found several farmers in the area that he contracted for custom hay stacking to which I also did at least eighty percent of it.

Overhead Electrical Wires

Now for some more interesting things that happened to me while using the Haybuster stacker. As I stated earlier the stacker was a tall and wide piece of equipment. Power lines hanging across roads were always a challenge to get under.

I had one stack that I made too large to move the arm low enough when hauling the stack to where it was to be unloaded. I thought that I had cleared the power line being almost past it. As I was starting to pick up speed, the bottom power line caught on a little corner of the arm. Not realizing that the line was caught, I kept driving. The line snapped sending sparks all over the place.

My first worry: would the dry stack of hay start on fire? I jumped from the tractor with the fire extinguisher.

While the haystack did not catch on fire the field did.

I was able to put the fire out while avoiding the live flopping power line. I was just extremely happy I did not burn up the hay stacker and tractor in that incident.

Next worry was telling Mom who was at home at the time what happened, then later, telling dad.

Faulk, Edmunds, and McPhearson (FEM) Power Cooperative sent someone out right away as that line cut power to some of our neighbors. They fixed the line that time by pulling the line a little tighter so it would be nearly a foot higher.

Wires and Recruiter

Another incident also involved power lines only this time I took down all five wires at once and killed all the electricity to our farm. How did it happen, you might ask?

It was the summer between my junior and senior year of high school. I was just unloading a stack of hay near the cattle yard when my youngest brother Kent came running out of the house screaming at me. He said I had a very important long-distance phone call and I needed to hurry up.

Since I had just unloaded the haystack, I hopped back in the tractor raising the flat bed as I rushed up to the house with stacker in tow--not realizing I had not yet lowered the chute arm on stacker.

I hit the five power lines snapping them with sparks flying everywhere. After making sure I could get out of the tractor. I rushed into the house to answer the phone.

I really did not feel sorry for that Army recruiter that was on the other end of the line. I bet he never forgot that phone call--I never will either.

I still thank God no one was outside at the time I hit those lines as it could have been fatal for anyone close.

The tractor saved me as the tires grounded the tractor, and the cab on the tractor had at least one power line bounce off it. Without that cab not sure if I would be writing this now.

Manure Rollover

Wintertime we put a front-end loader on the H tractor. With the loader we would fill a feeder hayrack two or three times a week letting the cattle feed from it.

One winter we had a snowstorm that made it next to impossible to get to the hay wagon. Instead, we fed the cattle in a little valley. It was not much of a hill but it gave the cattle a little more protection.

I would take a few loads of hay using the front-end loader on the H tractor down in the little valley and dump it for the cows for bedding and eating.

However, one morning I was in a hurry to finish up my chores before the school bus came and I left the loader a little too high as I was going down the side of the hill.

The front wheel of the tractor hit a frozen cow pie or cow manure causing the tractor to be off balance with the heavy load of hay.

Guess what happened next.

Yep, you are right the tractor rolled on its side down the hill.

I was able to jump off over the large tire as it started to roll, only leaving me a little sore from hitting the frozen ground. If I had not been able to jump, I would have been pinned under the tractor.

Electric Gate

Another incident that happened to me involved the H and front-end loader.

One year dad was upgrading the gate to the entrance of the pasture with a drive through electric gate and adding an electric fence.

We had a couple of cows that were not afraid of barb wire and were constantly breaking out.

It was a chilly Saturday morning; I think in October. My coveralls were in the washing machine and mom felt that my blue jeans weren't going to be warm enough. Mom wanted me to go out with dad that morning to help him install the new electric gate and electric fence.

Mom told me to try on her brand-new pair of overhauls that she had just boughten for herself. I remember telling her that I was afraid I would get them dirty right away and I did not think that I should wear them. Mom insisted.

I got them on and hurried to catch-up to dad to help him out. But, by the time I was able to get mom's coveralls on and out the door, dad had already taken the tractor over to the gate area with a roll of electric wire.

As soon as I got to the gate area, he asked me to lift him in the loader bucket. We had already installed two highline poles as posts for the electric gate and needed to string the wire across the gate area high enough for the tractor to go underneath without hitting it.

I stood on the hitch of the tractor, reached over to pull the lever to the hydraulics to lift the bucket up. I had dad where he needed to be and was about to climb into the driver's seat on the tractor.

Suddenly, the pant leg of the new coveralls bumped up against the power take off shaft that was spinning catching the new coverall material into it.

I was taken off my feet in a second and I braced myself the best I could as the power take off shaft stripped the brand-new coveralls off my body.

Dad was taken by surprise as much as I was. Being ten feet in the air, he could not do anything quickly to help me.

Somehow, I avoided major injury and after I was able to get myself free. I had welts from my ankles to my neckline from the material being ripped in shreds off of me.

I told dad I was ok, and he finished up quickly before I let him down.

Dad checked me over and said Zebras had nothing over me, then sent me back to the house stating he could finish on his own.

I was very worried about what mom was going to say as I knew she had saved up cream money to be able to get those new coveralls.

Instead, she was simply happy I was okay. She then tended to the wounds.

There was normally a shield that covered the power take off shaft, but Dad had taken it off because it was in the way when hooking up the grain grinder and he had not put it back on right away like it should have been.

For once it was not my fault, at least that was what I was thinking.

Neighbor's Brahman Cow

One time our neighbor down the road decided to give the Brahman cow breed a try. One of those cows always liked to get out of their pasture and into ours.

It was the spring and during calving season their Brahman cow decided to get into our pasture and have a calf. Dad and I went out in the pickup to drive the Brahman cow back home.

At that time, we did not know that she had just calved and when we got close enough to her, she charged the pickup putting a big dent in the side.

Dad told me we had to get her out of our pasture and the only way was to get the calf and put it in the box of the pickup and the cow would follow us. That was easier said than done.

I really did not want to get out of the truck, but I did. I climbed into the box of the truck and dad told me when he signaled, I was to jump out the box grab the calf and put it in the truck box and jump back in.

We circled the cow and the calf several times trying to separate the cow from the calf. When dad signaled me, I did just as he said—I got the calf and myself back in the truck box- just in time.

The cow hit the side of the truck so hard that I thought we were going to tip over. Dads' idea worked like a charm and the cow followed us all the way back to where she was supposed to be.

The calf, just being born, did not yet have leg strength; otherwise the plan would have never worked.

Imagine, making it back to our neighbors pasture, their Brahman cow chasing us, foaming at the mouth, and staying so close to our banged up pickup.

We had to unload that newborn calf.

Dad stepped on the gas petal to get some separation from the cow. When we finally had enough space, I hopped back out of the truck cab, and unloaded the calf just in time. That dangerous cow, trying to protect her calf, caught up to us again and we sped off.

Dad and our neighbor had a talk. He showed the neighbor the damage done to our truck and told him to be very careful with that breed of cows--especially during calving season. Then dad told him to fix his fence, as we didn't ever want to go through that again.

I do not remember ever having those neighbor's cows get out again. I believe he sold the Brahman cows he had that fall and replaced them with a milder black angus breed.

Naming Cows

We milked several cows. Every dairy cow had a name. This is just a few of the names I will never forget.

Jesse, I'm not really sure of what breed she was as she was sort of a salt and pepper color. Jesse was a kicker and we always had to put kickers (hobbles) on her to milk with machine or by hand without being kicked. She was a good milker otherwise we would not have messed with her.

Getting kickers on a cow that could kick like hell was always interesting. Kickers, two bent pieces of metal, was held together by a chain. Each metal piece would hook onto the cow's back legs. When the cow tried to kick, the chain would restrict the kick so the person milking would not get kicked as the cow could not swing either leg into kicking position.

It was always just as interesting taking the kickers off when done milking a hobbled cow.

Bettsy was a very large black and white Holstein. She was just the opposite of Jesse. She was gentle as can be.

Dotty was another large Holstein with spots.

Bottles you can guess why we gave her that name.

Blacky and Brownie were two more also very descriptive names of their body colors.

Heifer, she was a Herford and I think we must have been running out of names to come up with her name Heifer.

Milking

After we had finished milking the cows. The milk was hand carried up to the house in five-gallon pails. We had to carry them down to our basement.

The barn was 100 yards from the house. Hualing milk was done in several trips--it all depended on how many pails of milk we had during any given season.

The milk separator was kept in the basement where it was cool all year-round.

We would pour the milk into the top of the separator, start the separator, and watch as the cream would come out of one of the two spouts.

Cream, the lightest portion, would run into a clean pail. The milk that had the cream removed (skimmed milk) would come out of the second spout.

The skim milk would run back into the pail that was carried from the barn. Except what our family drank for milk, the skimmed milk was then carried back up the rock stairs out of the basement, and, depending on the time of the year, carried to the barn, or what we called the hog pasture roughly 300 yards from the farmhouse. The milk was mixed with grain and fed to the hogs and to pail calves (dairy cows' calves).

We always kept some milk for pasteurizing and drinking for ourselves which was collected in a clean smaller pail. We also kept enough cream for home use.

All the rest of the cream was taken into town and sold at the creamery in Ipswich.

After the creamery closed (probably from a lack of cream as small dairies became fewer), we washed and sanitized quart and pint jars selling cream to several individual customers—neighbors, and people in Ipswich.

About three miles from our farm, the Pembrook Hutterite Colony was our biggest cream customer. (See the **Cream Lady** story.)

Every day the separator would be taken apart and washed after every use so twice a day. This separator had many discs and other parts in it. In other words, it added more work washing and drying of all the other dishes, pots, pans, and milk pails.

We had plenty of dishes with a family of ten people in the house.

That was why we were strong kids in those days: each bale was handled perhaps up to ten times from baler to cattle, milking, carrying milk, and hand-feeding livestock. There was never any need to do weightlifting at the school gym.

Grain Harvesting

Our farm was a very diverse type of farming.

We grew corn and small grain crops to supply grains for wintering our livestock. Farm income was supplemented by selling excess grain we did not need for feeding cows, horses, hogs, or chickens. We also kept back high quality grains as seed for spring planting.

Our grain crop rotation would vary from year to year. We would have spring wheat, rye, oats, corn, and barley in our rotation for grains. Alfalfa and millet were used for forage.

Corn was mainly chopped for silage--the whole plant was used. Silage was an alternative to waiting for corn ears to dry down. The ears were picked with a one-row corn picker and it was shelled with a hand-cranked sheller (mentioned earlier). The hogs could eat corn off the cob. However, the cows were fed finely ground grains, including corn.

We had a pull-type combine that we pulled behind the H tractor. Our farming equipment was much smaller than what is used today.

For the most part, we were self-sufficient farmers.

Passed Out on Rye

One fall we had a great harvest of rye. The Rye was very tall, thick, and when swathed it had large heavy windrows of straw and grain.

The windrows were too large for our little Case combine in many areas. Harvesting became more labor intensive and required one person to stand on the head of the combine with a pitchfork to hold back some of the windrows as it fed into the combine--a very slow and dusty project.

Mom drove the tractor pulling the combine and I was the one that had to stand on the combine header making sure it did not feed to quickly and plug up the machine.

Imagine: after a few hours of this I was caked with layers of dust.

The bandana that I had over my face did not do enough to keep the dirt and dust from my lungs. I started to get dizzy.

We did not have that much left to finish up and all I could think of was let's get this done.

Suddenly, I heard the gears stop and mom yelling at me.

I did not know what was going on.

What happened was I passed out on the head of the combine from the dust and was laying with my left arm hanging over the head into the feeder part of the combine.

Mom saw me collapse and was able to shut everything down before I was fed into the combine.

I believe that harvest was the beginning cause of most of my lung issues I have had over the years...

...but at least I'm alive to talk about it.

Photo: our Coop grain swather made windrows allowing dry down before combining. This is a 1969 photo of my brother Gary fixing our swather.

First memories

Our first television: It sat on a little metal stand that swiveled. I think I thought the stand was as neat as the tv. I kept getting in trouble for turning it.

I had to be very young maybe two.

A plastic barn I am sitting on I received for Christmas.

Some of my first memories were major ones-- JFK assassination was one.

Mom was home with my baby brother Neal and me. I remember it was the first time I saw mom crying. I also remember asking her why she was crying because we were Republicans.

I was so small I think I took her by surprise with my question.

She said that didn't matter because Kennedy was our president and that it should not have happened.

There was the space shuttle to the moon--watching television and Neal Armstrong moon walking was memorable.

First time driving: I was four years old. Mom was in the hospital getting ready to have Neal. The rest of the kids were in school.

It was in February and a very cold winter day. The pickup wouldn't start for dad. I remember being bundled up in my warmest coat, cap, and mittens.

Dad tied a board to my foot to hold the clutch pedal down in the pick-up. I remember I could barely hold it down. I was not tall enough to sit decently on the seat. Even then, I could barely see out over the dashboard.

Dad then chained the pickup to the H-International tractor with a log chain. He told me to hold the petal down until he yelled then let it go. He said don't touch the other pedal. Try to hold the steering wheel straight.

Dad hopped on the tractor and started pulling the pick-up. The chain pulled tight; dad yelled, "Let it go!"

I let the pedal go, the pickup bounced and chugged and I fell over.

No luck on the first try.

Dad came back to the truck and got me set right again and ran back to tractor to try again. This time the truck started but kept moving forward. Dad somehow unhooked the pull chain from the tractor and drove it out of the way.

I was driving down our driveway on and off the road. Dad hopped off the tractor and ran to the truck and hopped in and stopped it before the truck hit a highline pole.

That was one of the most memorable happy days of my life at this point. I had just turned four two months earlier.

I was sure I was the youngest Wietgrefe kid ever to drive even though it was no more than a hundred yards.

Grandpa's Toenails

My grandfather, my dad's father, lived with us as long as I can remember. My grandmother passed away a year or so after I was born. Mom told many great stories of how mom loved grandma.

I mentioned in the beginning of this book that grandpa was crippled from a car accident. He walked with a cane all the time and Grandpa was pretty handy with that cane at times.

He would turn his cane upside down and hook onto your leg just to tease you or to get your attention.

I wrote about doing chores at a young age. One of my chores was to take care of grandpa. We would get him water and snacks during the day.

One job I hated was clipping grandpa's toenails. Some of grandpas toe's turned in and I had to try to straighten it out the best I could and clip the nail.

First we would wash and dry his feet. His feet often had a good strong foot odor. This was a weekly task.

I don't think there were too many six-to-eight-year-olds that have done this task for anyone. I could be wrong, but I sure didn't think so back then.

Grandpa's Drink

One particular story I remember involved Neal and grandpa.

I was out in the field with Mom raking hay and Neal and grandpa were keeping each other company.

Grandpa had asked Neal to get him a glass of water and Neal did so. This happened a couple of times before Mom, and I got back home from the field.

Mom realized that she did not put a pitcher of water out for grandpa to fill his glass. Mom asked grandpa how he had a full glass of water left by his chair. Grandpa said he asked Neal and Neal filled the glass for him.

This really went through mom's mind as Neal was not tall enough to get water and the kitchen stool did not look like it had moved.

Mom took Neal into the other room and asked him about grandpa's water. Neal said, "It was easy mom. I just dipped the glass in the big white bowl in the bathroom and there was plenty of water."

I think mom was about to faint and I broke out laughing so hard my stomach hurt.

I don't think that we ever told grandpa he was drinking toilet water.

Grandpa Fish & Games

Grandpa also liked to go fishing when he could.

We carried a very long, I think sixteen foot bamboo pole for him. Dad would tie it onto the passenger side of the car to the mirror and door handles.

I don't know how long the string was, but I remember it being yellow in color and thick.

Grandpa liked to take leftover roast beef or chicken meat and put it on a hook and toss the line out with a big bobber on it.

I remember grandpa caught some pretty big northern pike and catfish using that pole.

Grandpa loved to play cards with us kids when we were little. Some family game time we played Crazy 8, Slap Jack, Concentration, Go Fish, and Whist.

When he didn't want to play, he loved to make us play fifty-two pick-up. He told mom, "The kids loved that game."

Overall grandpa was good to us kids.

Car—First Accident

The first car accident I had was driving home from school. I was on the gravel road and a deer jumped out of the ditch in front of me. I swerved to not hit it and went into the ditch.

The ditch in that area was deep. It's dead stop embankment came almost to the top of the hood of the pickup.

I was banged up with bruises only, but I was only about a mile and a half from home.

The truck was not going to get out on its own.

I ended up walking the rest of the way home. Dad and I took the tractor and chain to pull it out of the ditch. Lucky, we just needed to patch up the radiator and fix a couple of dents, nothing major on the truck.

I remember dad telling me that if a deer ran in front of me again, I should just hit it. From skids on the road, he said I was lucky I did not roll the truck.

Next Car Accident

The next accident happened after I moved to Brookings, South Dakota. I was out hunting with my Datson pickup early one morning on a gravel road. I was not familiar with that area. I was driving east and going up and down hills. When I came to the top of one hill, another pickup was coming toward me. I pulled to the side of the road without slowing down much as the pickup passed by me.

The sun popped up over the hill. I had no idea that the road had a sharp turn right on the other side of the hill. With the sun shining straight in my eyes I drove off the road through a barb wire fence and ended up at the bottom of the hill in someone's pasture. I was able to stop before going into a big drop off into a creek bed.

The pickup did have damage--only cosmetic. I was able to turn around and go back up the hill to where I went through the fence and made it back on the road. I parked and was trying to put the fence back together as there were cattle in the pasture. The owner of the pasture showed up. I explained what had happened. That farmer was very generous and told me I was very lucky. A few years back the same thing happened to a young couple, but they never made it back.

He said there was a Curve Ahead sign placed up after that incident. When we looked for the sign, it was lying in the ditch. Someone else knocked it over. We fixed the fence together and put the sign back up before I left. I never drove that road again.

Barn Fire Bare

Driving home from Brookings late one Friday, I noticed a fire in a farmer's barn. I quickly turned back to the farmer's place and knocked on the door.

As I stated earlier it was late, I think around midnight.

I really was not prepared for what came to the door.

The farmer was bare ass naked with a shotgun in his hand.

"What the hell do you want?" He yelled at me.

I said your barn is on fire. He laid down his gun, put on cowboy boots, grabbed a fire extinguisher, and ran out toward the barn.

No coat or clothes. It was winter and cold outside but that did not matter to that farmer.

The two of us were able to put out the fire. A heater, to keep his piglets from freezing, started the straw bedding on fire. We caught it in time. Another 15 to 20 minutes later, I think the barn, hogs and all would have been gone.

The guys wife came out while we were working on the fire with some clothes and a coat for the farmer.

I was sure happy she came out with clothes on.

Both were quite big people.

Asleep at the Wheel

After the barn fire, I left the farmer's place around 1:30 a.m. and with a roughly two-and-a-half-hour drive ahead.

I made it near the Geditz farm on Highway 45 before falling asleep at the wheel.

I drove in the ditch over two approaches and woke up before dropping in the gully. I had to back up to the last approach to get back on the highway.

At that point I was just a little over a mile from home as the crow flies and less than three miles of road to home.

Water Skiing Fish Trap

I was with some close friends water skiing on Pelican Lake near Watertown, South Dakota. I have to admit that I really was not that great of a skier as I had only done it once or twice before.

It took me quite a few tries before I finally got up. I was staying up well as we scooted around the lake. One time I came close to skiing into another boat coming from the opposite direction as it came way too close to our boat.

My boat driver made a swing closer to shore to get out of the way of the oncoming boat. I caught the wakes from both boats. Somehow, I managed to keep my balance and kept going.

Now, closer to shore, my right ski went under a wire that was attached to a fish trap. My ski was cut in half--just in front of the ski's foothold.

I went tumbling across the top of the water rolling toward the shoreline. Two fortunate things happened then:

1.) I was very fortunate the shoreline was filled with a lot of reeds as they slowed me down before actually hitting shore.

2.) I still had a right foot.

Quieting the Van

To save some money before moving to Bismarck, North Dakota I sold my truck and bought an old Ford Econoline van.

The van had two bucket seats with the motor sitting between them. The rest of the van was just a cargo van with nothing else inside.

I had moved in with my sister, Susan, and her husband Rick Williams. I rented the basement from them.

While I lived there, I bought some paneling and carpet and did my best to make the van a little quieter for driving.

The bridge I had to drive over daily to get to work in Mandan was a metal bridge with grid plate base. When I drove over that bridge the sound was deafening in that old van before I insulated and paneled it.

There was a Neuschwander gathering for an Anniversary party in Thief River Falls, Minnesota that I decided to go to. (Neuschwander was my paternal grandmother's name.)

I bought a huge forty-eight pound watermelon to take along. I placed it just behind the motor. The melon was blocked from rolling back with a coffee can and a lead weight that I had made from melting down a couple of old car batteries. The weight was shaped in a tuna can. With carpeted floor, the can did not move, and held the watermelon in place.

Another Roll or Two

I was on the road through North Dakota and Minesota for several hours driving. The speed limit at that time was 65 miles-per-hour. I did not have cruise control so I'm sure I went a little faster from time to time.

I think I must have been falling asleep at the wheel.

All I remember was one second I was going along fine. When I came to a curve in the highway the steering wheel seemed to me it would not turn the wheels.

I went off the curve and the van flipped end over end twice and ended up with me looking at the ground through what used to be a windshield.

As soon as I knew I was going to roll the van, I reached over to the passenger seat laying my body over the top of the motor and held onto the passenger seat.

The van was stopped by a highline pole right down the middle of the top of the van. The roof caved in around the pole with my back right up against the roof and my belly on top of the motor.

Like all my other accidents, I knew for sure that I had a guardian Angel with me.

After getting my wits about me I tried to get out of the doors. They were jammed shut.

I remember having a hard time getting my lap seat belt off. The van was before shoulder harness belts.

The only way out was through the back of the van which was facing the sky. The back doors were gone.

I managed to climb up and out, having to fall to the ground.

A car had stopped on the highway with a lady behind the wheel. She was in shock as she thought that she had just witnessed someone getting killed.

Remember that watermelon I mentioned at the beginning? When the van started to roll, the watermelon rolled up over the engine and my back. It took out the windshield of the van leaving a watermelon splatter all over.

That watermelon looked like blood from a distance.

The lady in shock could not speak and was shaking.

Not knowing what else to do I hopped behind the wheel of her car and drove her to the hospital which was around 15 to 20 miles away from the accident.

From the hospital, I called the Neuschwanders and they came to get me.

At that point I only had minor cuts and bruises. The lady recovered and she was released to go home.

Two of my cousins went out with a truck and tractor to get the van and I sat and visited for a while.

I was then asked if I needed some rest and was going to be shown the bedroom where I was to stay the weekend with them.

I made it halfway up the staircase and my legs gave out on me. While rolling down the stairs my jacket got caught on the railing brace and ripped a big hole in it.

I received a gash on my head and cut my arm falling down those stairs.

I was asked if I needed to go back to the hospital. I refused.

I was put in a recliner where I fell asleep for a couple of hours before finally seeing the bedroom.

While I slept, the guys came back with the van.

That lead weight they found embedded in the roof just above the windshield where my rearview mirror used to be. First, they could not believe I made it out of it alive. Secondly, they could not figure out how I was able to get out at all.

Broadsided 1967 Chevy

I had three more car accidents after the van one. All three cars were totaled and all three involved other drivers running stop signs.

First of the three accidents I was living in Bismarck, North Dakota. A young mother went through a stop sign and broadsided me.

Her car hit me on the driver side of my pickup.

I was traveling at 55 miles an hour and not sure how fast she was going.

I had fixed up an old 1967 Chevy pick-up. That truck only had lap seatbelt. I hit my head on the door frame and was knocked unconscious.

Ambulances seemed like they were there in seconds.

Both the driver and passenger in the other car were taken by ambulance to the hospital. I was also taken in by ambulance. I had a few stiches put in on my head. After a few head scans, I was released.

I was not allowed to find out any information on the other two people. One was a child around a year old.

I relived this accident many times in my head and finally decided there was nothing I could have done to avoid it.

Broke Fire Hydrant

The second accident happened in the town of North Branch, Minnesota. As I was entering the town, the speed limit changed to forty-five miles-per-hour.

I noticed the car about to hit me had stopped at the stop sign as I was approaching the intersection. The driver of the car stepped on the gas pedal to go through the intersection not seeing me coming.

She hit the passenger's side of my vehicle causing me to go into a spin. My vehicle ended up on the curb and broke off a fire hydrant.

My air bags deployed. I was ok. The lady that hit me was driving a large LTD limited. She was eighty-seven-years-old and just did not see me.

She had some bruises and the police made sure she was taken to the hospital to be checked out.

Four Car Sandwich

The third accident happened in Eden Prairie, Minnesota. The speed limit was forty-five-miles-an-hour. I was approaching a signal light when suddenly the car in front stomped on its brakes as the light turned yellow. I quickly stopped and avoided hitting the car in front of me.

The car behind me did not slow down. It hit the rear end of my car with the car behind him creating a car sandwich. Of course, the car behind me was smashed between my car and the car behind it. The driver of the car that hit me was removed, put on a stretcher and was ambulanced out.

The car that hit me was going at least forty-five miles an hour at the point of impact. I actually think he was going much faster. Because I still had my foot on the brake. I did not hit the car in front of me very hard, though the back seat and trunk of my car was pushed forward against my driver's seat.

While this accident sounded mild compared to the other accidents I was in, I did receive a good whiplash injury to my neck. I went to a chiropractor for several treatments and physical therapy for months afterwards. This accident caused more damage to me than all the others put together.

Both the second and third accidents were with company cars. I was working for Supervalu® at the time as a Meat Specialist driving from store to store doing my job. I put on sixty-to-eighty-thousand miles a year driving company cars.

Neighbor's Farm Accidents

Growing up on a farm there are so many adventures and hazards that kids growing up in cities or towns do not have a clue. Accidents can happen at a moment's notice.

Our closest neighbor to the west of our place was just a mile away. One of their sons had his arm badly broken and skin and muscle ripped off him in a grain auger. He was very lucky to survive as he lost most of his blood when it happened.

Another neighbor to the north of our farm had two boys. While they were only five and six-years-old, the younger boy grabbed a pitchfork and poked out his older brothers eye with it.

Terrible accident. He was fitted with a glass eye and had to learn how to take it out and clean it at that young age.

When I was in high school there was a farmer that lost his life to a hay baler getting caught in the feeder end and partially baled. I do not remember his name or how far away from our farm it happened, but it made a very big impression on me.

That accident confirmed to me that I did not want to be a farmer all my life.

Siblings

My siblings: Top left to right: Susan, Gary, Mark; Second row left to right: Wayne, me, and Neal.

Kent, the last of my siblings, was born in 1966 and held by our father.

Neighbors Help Harvest

While mom was hospitalized in 1967 our neighbors showed up in force to help with harvest.

Granary

It was a family project taking down our old wooden grain bin. Dismantled in 1969, our parents had everyone involved.

Good wood was saved for multiple other farm projects.

When younger, us kids used the old building to play Anti-I-Over. That involved throwing a ball over the roof and another sibling trying to catch it on the other side.

Handling Chicks

Wayne (right) and I (left) are having fun cleaning chickens.

We grew big birds and also had nice hair at the time.

New Shed

In 1972 we built our machine shed. Dad led the project. I very much enjoyed helping with this construction as I learned a lot about carpentry work from my father.

Joshua Tree

Over Thanksgiving 1973, I was introduced to Joshua trees. I told you I liked to climb on things as a kid. I am in the tree. Also pictured left to right: Neal, Kent, Mom, and Gary.

Gary was returning from an Air Force base in Italy and was being restationed in Japan. While on military leave, he cashed in his plane ticket and used that money for gas during the 1973 Mideast Oil Crisis. We drove him from South Dakota to a California Air Force base where Mark was stationed. It was my first time in multiple states. Great trip. Thanks Gary!

Our Farm House

This was our farmhouse. The right side (ranch-style) was added to the original house in 1958. It was built as our grandparent's place. It had two bedrooms and our first indoor

bathroom.

After my grandmother passed away in 1959, it

became my grandfather's side of the house. Meanwhile, the two-story (west) side with two bedrooms upstairs was where my parents, six siblings, and I lived.

Eventually, my parents moved to one of grandfather's bedrooms allowing Susan to have her own room and the six of us boys shared the other upstairs bedroom.

Susan Graduates

I am so proud of my sister Susan. She graduated from Lab Tech school in Minneapolis, Minnesota. (Susan is front right.) This is just a speculation on my part...I always thought she went into medical school because she thought I was going to need her to help me out after some kind of accident. She had plenty of practice before then.

Brothers Serve Country

Gary 1971

U.S. Air Force

Mark 1972

U.S. Air Force

Kent 1986

South Dakota

Air National Guard

Three of my brothers served our country. Gary and Mark joined the Air Force during the Vietnam War. Kent joined the South Dakota Air National Guard while in college. I salute each of you and thank you for your service.

Dairy Farming

Kent is driving our three-wheel cart (below) and I am

just having some fun with Kent as I was popping my bike wheel into the box. I have many stories about my bike--like jumping our station wagon in our front yard and jumping over the stock dam just to name a couple.

I graduated from high school in 1976. That day and evening, I borrowed the folk's car. I stayed out all night partying with classmates and got home at four a.m. Mom was sitting on the front doorstep with a broom in her hand. I didn't know if she was just sweeping the steps at that ungodly hour, or she had other things in mind.

I hopped out of my parent's car tossed mom the keys and told her I had to get to work. I jumped in my car and left. It was my first day working for a dairy farmer near Roscoe-- about twenty miles away. I was told to start at six a.m. I had my clothes already packed in my car and the things I needed. I was sure mom was mad at me for staying out so late, but as a teenager, I really didn't care at that point. The farmer paid me $500 a month plus board and room. That was a lot of money for me at the time. I believe I was milking 160 head of cows in the morning and late afternoons. Milking started at 5:30 a.m.

and 4:30 p.m. It took roughly two and half hours to milk during each time frame.

After having a very good breakfast each morning I would go and work in his fields picking rock with a rock picker. I thought that was something. On our farm when picking rocks, we did it by hand throwing the rocks in the front-end loader of the tractor as we walked the fields.

During the three or four months that I worked on that farm I had a couple of close calls. Once I was charged by a cow that just had a calf. The truck I was driving started on fire from a squirrel nest on the engine. In both cases I was able to avoid serious injury.

I am standing by my first car, a 1940 Special Deluxe Chevy. Dad's motorcycle is on the left, and our red cowbarn is in the background. The gate (as in Pearl-Gate) is hidden

between our yard light pole and the barn. An old one-room schoolhouse (white building) we moved to our farmstead and converted it into a butchering building where I began learning my career.

Concrete Foreman

Dad told me of a job in Bismarck, North Dakota working concrete construction. I applied and was hired. That job paid really well. At the time, my sister, Susan, and her husband, Rick, lived in Bismarck. They offered me their basement to rent. That worked out really well for me.

I had only been on that job three months and was promoted to be foreman of a six-man crew. I was only nineteen years old at the time. It was a huge responsibility. We measured and poured house foundations as well as basement floors, sidewalks, and any other sites that used concrete.

One of my crew lost his driver's license. He was a severe alcoholic living in a hotel. I had to drive to pick him up in the morning and take him back home in the evening. He was a very good worker, but some mornings were tough.

We worked four 10-hour days so he would try to be sober during workdays and binge on his days off.

Within a few short months with this job, I picked up my crew and went to the office. That was the routine; I would pick up our work orders for the week and head to the location.

The office door was locked. There was a big note on it saying. WE WENT OUT OF BUISNESS! I and my crew were shocked, as were the other two crews that came after us. None of us had a clue. It took nearly four months to get our last paycheck.

Trained as a Butcher

Since I did not have a job, Gary asked me to move to Brookings, South Dakota where he was going to college after the Air Force. Gary owned a three-bedroom trailer house and had been renting two of the bedrooms to college friends the previous semester.

Gary had to go to military intelligence training school in Colorado and would be gone for a few months. He asked if I would watch over his trailer rent free while he was gone. I could look for a job.

I went to the Brookings Job Service office, filled out a bunch of papers, and they said if I was interested the local locker plant was looking for a butcher.

The State would pay half my salary to the owner if I was willing to go through a three-year training program called Butcher All Around.

The name of the place was Artz Lockers and Water Softeners. I accepted as I was to get formal training and receive pay. That sounded like a rather good deal to me.

The butcher all around program required training in all aspects of the locker meat business. It was a steppingstone for me to go into business on my own after I completed the three-year program.

During that time, I worked my way through the business. Once I mastered a skill, I moved on to the next skill set.

I started out on the slaughter floor. We would slaughter on average seven head of cattle and ten hogs per day with occasional sheep or two mixed in.

Slaughtering was not just killing the animals it was gutting, skinning, and quartering them.

My mentor (Henry) and I were kept very busy. It took a while for me to get used to the smell, blood, and all that came with that job.

One day a week we did not slaughter. That day was set aside for prepping and smoking hams, bacon, sausages, and making dried beef.

Every morning before we did the slaughtering, we would take items out to the smoker, putting them on drying racks in a cooler and put more items in the smoker for the day.

I very much enjoyed that part of the job learning the total curing process for each item. The slaughtering and smoking job training was the entire first year.

Buffalo Bull

One day we had a big buffalo bull come to the plant. He was brought in a semi-trailer with the bull having the full run of the trailer.

Though our holding pens were concrete blocks with steel pipe doors, my boss felt the buffalo would rip pens apart.

We used a 22-caliber rifle to kill slaughter animals shooting a plastic bullet. Always done at close range, it worked well with cattle and hogs, but a big buffalo I wasn't sure it would go through the thick scull.

I told my boss I had my 243 rifle in my truck. We were all concerned about using that gun as the locker plant was in the town of Brookings and if I missed the bullet could bounce off of the wall or go through the semi-trailer.

We decided to go ahead with the 243. The buffalo was running back and forth through the semi-trailer getting quite worked up.

A plan was set. When the trailer door opened, I was to jump out in front of the buffalo and shoot it before it made it into the plant. The driver would not allow me to shoot it on the trailer, so I had to wait until the bull started into the plant.

Nervous. I had very little room for error. The semi doors were opened. The bull ran to the end of the trailer, stopped short, and turned back and ran to the front of trailer.

He then charged toward me. I fired as his front feet hit our ramp coming in the door. He fell with such momentum that his whole body kept coming right at me. My only option was to jump up. The bulls head hit the concrete block wall that was right behind me.

I landed on his front shoulders. I immediately turned putting another bullet in the back of his head to make sure he stayed down. My hands were shaking. I was covered with sweat from that frightening experience. When the bulls head hit the concrete block wall it put a crack in the wall that went all the way to the ceiling.

The bull was so big our hoist struggled to lift him in the air. That ten-foot-high mechanical lift went to the ceiling and the buffalo head and front legs were still on the floor.

We never took another buffalo after that one.

Sailing Knife

The second year I worked in the cutting room, cutting and packaging the meat. That was nothing for me as I had learned the process from my mother on the farm.

However, one day while dropping a hind quarter on the butcher block table I had not noticed that one of the other cutters left a knife lay on the block. When I dropped the quarter on the block it hit the knife and it went sailing through the air--just missing one of our cutters and stuck into the wall.

I See

Another day while I was cleaning our holding cooler. We would wash the bright white walls to give the coolers a thorough cleaning. Although in training, I was not informed I had to shut off the ultraviolet lights before starting. Those lights worked to kill bacteria that can grow without them.

Cleaning the cooler took at least an hour. When I came out of the cooler my eyes were burning and I could not see clearly.

My boss took me to the eye doctor right away. The doctor flushed my eyes out, put drops in my eyes, and covered them with gauze. I could not see at all with the bandages over my eyes. I went nearly a week blinded with bandages.

My boss's quick action saved my eyesight. When I returned to work big, laminated signs were on all the cooler doors that stated, "Shut off ultraviolet lighting if in cooler more than five minutes at a time."

Business of Butchering

After the ultraviolet light incident, I started working in the office with my boss (Sam).

Sam had me work with customers and taught me the financial workings of his business. Remember the name of the plant was Artz Locker and Water Softeners.

Sam taught me all about the soft water business as well.

I worked with his one and only delivery and repair man. I covered for him when he was on vacation.

I delivered soft water tanks to many homes including several farm homes.

Dog Softener

I remember one farmhouse in particular. The softener was in the basement. It was snowing and was a little slippery. I had not been to this house before but was told where the softener hook up was and thought it was no big deal.

I wore a strap around my shoulder to carry the cylinder tank which weighed roughly eighty pounds. I carried the tank in front of me over to the house where the trap doors were covered with snow. I set the tank down, brushed off as much snow as I could and flung the doors open.

To my surprise the basement steps were old car and tractor batteries. The batteries were tipped upside down so the posts were facing downward.

I thought that was interesting. Wondered what the basement was like?

I picked up the tank and started to go down the battery steps. They were very slippery with the snow on my boots. I went flying down the steps with the tank on my chest.

I stood up and the basement was very dark. My flashlight I carried while on that job had fallen out of my pocket when I fell. I could not find a light switch on the wall.

Once again, I took the tank out of the strap, set it down and, on my knees, started to feel around for the flashlight. All of a sudden, I felt a warm breath on my face.

I could not see it, but I knew it was a big dog.

At that point I found the flashlight. I turned it on and in front of me was a dog the size of a bear. The dog was black as can be.

He licked my face as I was still on my knees, and I was so happy he was friendly.

I shined the flashlight around looking for a light switch. There was none to be found. I did see where the tank hookup was, so I carried the tank over to the spot and hooked it up. After putting the old tank in my sling I headed for those battery steps.

The dog was by my side the whole time. I did see that he had food and water placed down there for him but without light that bothered me.

I made my way up those steps holding onto the wall all the way up. The dog did not even attempt those steps.

I closed the doors, went back to the truck and wrote a note stating tank was changed and that I enjoyed their dog. I posted it to the front door of the house and left.

My boss received a phone call before I was back to the office with a big thank you.

I was just happy they were back home knowing the dog must have been taken care of.

Winner Loser

After finishing and receiving my certificate of accomplishment for the three-year Butcher All Around program, Gary and I saw that a locker plant was for sale in Winner, South Dakota.

Winner is west of the Missouri River in southcentral part of our state. It was very nice cattle country. We thought it was a great opportunity to get into business.

I quit working at the Artz locker. I had purchased my own trailer by that time, and I moved it to Winner.

Our agreement with the owner of that locker was that I would work with them for free for a month prior to us making the commitment to buy.

It was a good thing we made that agreement. Though they had a great operation, the roof on the building was in bad shape and needed at least $100,000 repair which was far out of our financial scope. I figured that out in the first couple of weeks.

I backed out of our commitment and I was once again without a job.

I was living in a town that more than likely would not like me for backing out of buying the locker plant.

I called Susan and asked if I could rent her basement again and looked for a job up in Bismarck. She and Rick said yes, and I sold my trailer in Winner and moved back to Bismarck.

I found a job with Dan's Supervalu® in Bismarck as a meat cutter within a day or two after moving.

Opportunities abound. We just need to look around and take advantage of them. No matter what age, things happen.

Remembering Dad

Dad always had a smile on his face and tool in hand. Dad passed away in 1980 during heart surgery in Minneapolis, Minnesota. That was a tremendous loss, he was only 51 years old.

Cattle Drives

I always enjoyed cattle drives. On one drive I found my dad's wristwatch he lost two years prior on a cattle drive. It still worked when it was wound. Dad wore it proudly after that.

Potato Harvest

It was a family activity getting ready for potato harvest. In 1969 there were four rows like those in the photo which we picked all up by hand after our antique potato digger brought them to the surface. The rows were a quarter mile long. We ate a lot of potatoes  that year with extras to plant the following year. Nothing went to waste. Any extra cut and scarred were fed to the pigs.

Best Decision

The very best decision I ever made was in 1980. Jeanne said yes. I met Jeanne at Dan's Supervalu®. She worked in the Deli and I was in the meat department.

Jeanne and I hit it off right away as both of us went through very serious hospitalizations as kids. Jeanne had

cancer in her kidney and lost one kidney. She was only seven years old at the time.

The following year she had a cancerous brain tumor that was radiated. She was very ill those two years, and many prayers were prayed for her. I was told by her mother that there was strong concern to whether she would pull through.

Jeanne is a survivor much like me. By far, that was not what attracted me to her. She is gorgeous and has the best giving, kindest heart you will ever meet. She was also a fantastic cook. What more could I ask for in a wife?

Jeanne's mother and father treated me like one of their own as well. I asked her to marry me after dating only three months. We were married in 1981.

Honeymoon Changed

Prior to getting married we planned a honeymoon in Hawaii. Since both of us had good jobs, we were sure we could make it work.

One month before we were married Jeanne was laid off work.

I really wanted to take her to Hawaii--that was her dream. We both had newer cars with payments and just could not afford to do that honeymoon without her having a job.

We had to cash in the tickets we had purchased. We instead honeymooned in the Black Hills of South Dakota. Not quite Hawaii, but (well before Airbnb's) we found a very nice little A framed cottage with peacocks waking us up in the morning sitting on our deck.

They spread their feathers for us and made everything seem like we were really meant for each other.

Mice Move

I was offered a job as meat manager at a Jack & Jill store in Hettinger, North Dakota about six months after we were married.

Money was very tight, but we made the move from Bismarck to Hettinger.

Little did I know that the house we found to rent was infested with mice.

We had some new furniture that we bought with the money we received as wedding gifts. I really did not want the mice to get into the furniture. So, being a hunter, I spent the first two nights patching holes and trapping mice.

I went to work the day after we moved. Fortunately, Jeanne did not know about the mice until a day or two later.

She just thought I was restless because of the move and job change. I did not go to bed until 2:30-to-3 a.m.

The job was going well, however Jeanne was pregnant and she had never lived anywhere other than Bismarck. She was getting very homesick.

I saw that a new grocery store was opening in Bismarck called Holiday. I decided to apply for the meat managers position because I knew we could not afford to move back without that salary. To my surprise, I got the job. Jeanne and I were only in Hettinger for three months.

Cash Strapped

Jeanne and I struggled to pay our bills at that time. We did not have the cash to move again.

I was also going to become a father soon. I needed to do something.

I sold my motorcycle, large shop equipment (radio arm saw, table saw, and air compressor), and worst of all my beloved guns.

The sale of those items paid the bills that needed to be covered right away, but it was not enough.

I needed two months' rent up front for Bismark and I was still $300 short after figuring moving expenses.

I bit my tongue, swallowed my pride and called mom to ask for help.

I only asked for what was needed for our rent, nothing extra, just $300.

That hurt me more to ask for help than anything I went through before. That just was not me.

No Pulse

In 1982 our first child was born. That baby had my heart the moment I saw the very first ultrasound.

Jeanne and I were not sure that we would be able to have children because of her past.

We prayed a lot for her and our baby to come.

When Jeanne was in labor for nearly twenty-four hours, there was a moment when the nurse could not find the baby's pulse.

That scared me so bad that I passed out in the maternity room.

I woke up with more nurses around me then Jeanne.

I was so embarrassed, and the nurse was so apologetic to me for not having the monitor in the right place.

They made me eat and drink something. With all the excitement, I had forgotten that I had not eaten any food for a day and half.

The baby was born, and Jeanne was OK. That was really all that mattered to me. We named our baby girl Kayla Lea.

She was the cutest little thing with thin light blond hair weighing seven pounds and four ounces.

Cemetery

Besides taking on the big responsibility of my new job, I had five employees under me. I needed a little more income.

I asked my father-in-law if he needed any extra help at the cemetery. He was the superintendent for St. Mary's cemetery at the time. He said yes and I was very happy I had asked.

I could work for him on my days off from my regular job which was almost always Tuesday and Wednesday. Being in the grocery business, weekends were always very busy, and I needed to be at the store during that time. Having a weekend off was rare.

Working at the cemetery I dug graves, assisted with burials, mowed, and trimmed around the head stones.

I was also taught how to level headstones without breaking them. I leveled too many to remember.

I have to say I did not realize all the work that went into taking care of a cemetery.

The money I made from working on my days off for the cemetery, I was able to pay mom back right away even though she said I did not have to. It just made me feel better.

Growing Tumor and Baby

A year later our second child was born. This pregnancy also came with some challenges. Jeanne had a fibroid tumor that was growing faster than the baby.

The tumor had to be removed halfway through the pregnancy because if it was not removed, it could kill our baby.

Once again, many prayers were made.

When it came time for the baby to be born labor was not nearly as long as it was for Kayla. We had a nice big baby boy and named him Wade Wesley.

Wade was born with a thick head of hair and weighed eight pounds nine and a half ounces. He definitely took after his mother's side.

Once again Jeanne, being my rock, came through that doing well. I could not have been any happier than that.

Steal and Fire

I managed that meat department for eight years. I was always one of the top meat managers for Holiday.

The company operated over thirty stores--mainly in the Twin Cities area in Minnesota.

During those eight years I only had to fire two cutters--both for stealing.

They were very good meat cutters. I hated to do it, but they had to be let go.

I had a very good crew working for me. Three of them were with me from the beginning and still with me at the end of my time with this company.

Steel Sliver and Seizure

I was working in my garage grinding metal. A steel sliver flew under my glasses and into my eye. Jeanne drove me to the ER. At the time, our kids were two and three-years-old. Jeanne dropped me off at the ER doors and I walked in. I was taken into a room, to have the sliver removed from my eye. Jeanne parked the car before coming into the ER.

Jeanne was carrying Wade and Kayla was holding her hand as they walked into the ER. Right after the three of them had walked into the ER Wade had a seizure in Jeannes' arms. Wade scared the heck out of Jeanne. His eyes rolled back in his head and lost consciousness. Jeanne ran to a nurse and was immediately taken to a room. I was unaware of Wades situation at first.

The sliver was removed and my eye was covered with a patch. When I came out of my room, I could not find Jeanne and the kids.

Wade's admitting nurse knew who I was looking for as soon as I told her. I was sure glad that if Wade was going to have a seizure, he was in the right place at the right time.

Wade was having trouble with his ears and ear infections. He already had tubes in his ears. The hospital kept Wade overnight to do further testing. What happened? Wade developed a blood infection and was treated immediately.

Garage Door

At thirteen-months apart, many thought we had twins. Wade was the same size or a little bit bigger than Kayla at age one.

One day while I was working at the cemetery, Jeanne was babysitting for my brothers-in-law's two kids ages ten and eleven. Our neighbor was at home working in his garage right next to ours. He had a boy who was six. All the kids were playing together near the garages. Kayla, our daughter, age five climbed up on the pick-up tail gate of my neighbors truck.

She thought she was big enough to close the garage door for him. She jumped grabbing the garage door handle and fell to the floor. The door fell on her—very fast. There was no garage door openers at that time. Kayla hit her head on the floor hard with the door on top of her.

Jeanne called 911. The ambulance rushed her to the hospital emergency room right away. Jeanne was in a dilemma with extra kids and me not being at home. Our neighbors watched the other kids till they could be picked up.

Jeanne followed the ambulance to the hospital and called her father and brother. Her Dad told me what happened and her brother quickly appeared to pick up his kids. I rushed to the hospital. Kayla had a very serious head injury and was in the hospital for several days. Prayers again, more people than I even knew had prayed for her recovery. She recovered, kept her beautiful smile with no long-term complications.

Suit, Tie and Automation

I wanted a job change. An opportunity came up with Supervalu®. I decided to apply for a buying position at their warehouse in Bismarck. To my surprise they hired me right away. It was an office job sitting behind a desk in suit and tie.

It was not really my style of job as I was more of a hands-on and more physical worker. I could not afford to turn down the pay and benefits the job had offered.

Having two kids at the time and plenty of medical bills piling up, I once again did odd jobs on my time off of my regular job. I had to lower the never-ending bills.

I did a large job painting the outside of our condo association garages. I believe there were thirty-six total. Then I shingled houses after a hailstorm on evenings and weekends.

With the new job I had forgotten what it was like to be able to take the weekend and the holidays off. It was rare for me to have a holiday off at the store level. That part in particular made the new job much better.

When I first took the job, I started buying a little over nine-hundred items for the warehouse. They were mostly processed lunchmeats and some frozen items.

With each purchase I made, we had what we called price cards. The price card had a spot for the item--name on top, columns below for date of purchase, cost, and warehouse selling price.

I was constantly filling out those cards while buying several items every day. For automation, we had key punch personal that would enter my data into the computer in the computer room.

After all data was key punched, the price cards were sent back to me. I would file those cards and send a bunch more to be punched. It was quite the process the first few years. Everything was done on Disk Operating Systems (DOS) computer program with floppy disks.

Everything ran extremely slow compared to today's computers. As computers started to get better, I no longer had to fill out price cards. I just had to enter the data into the system myself. What an improvement for a much faster and smoother process.

Price cards were the boring part of the job. I made the decisions on what new items the warehouse should carry which included having meetings with several different vendors weekly.

The vendors would bring in samples of the new products. I would make suggestions to my boss, and he had final approval if we were going to handle the new item or not.

I learned quite a bit about negotiation skills during that process. I was able to take the samples home. With our medical bills, free food was another tremendous benefit.

I also had to sell and make sure the products I purchased were not in our warehouse more than a week or two at the most.

All items I purchased had expiration dates and our retail stores also needed to have the longest dates possible. Stores were guaranteed three weeks of dating, so they had time to sell each product.

I would walk through the warehouse every morning before going to my desk. I would check all the dates and make sure the warehouse guys were rotating products according to dating. If I saw something that was not right, I went back at my desk, and typed up a memo to the warehouse manager to get things corrected. I did that every day for ten years.

Supervalu® did a major conversion and my job ended in Bismarck.

Supervalu® Move

I applied for a Meat Specialist job with Supervalu® in Hopkins, Minnesota and I was hired. The Meat Specialist job was to sell Supervalu® meat programs and products while maintaining good relationships with independent retailers.

My job involved training better management techniques to retail store managers. I also trained meat cutters on new cuts of meat. To improve their sales, I also reset their meat cases to the newest styles or seasonal sets.

The new job came with a company car and many hours of driving between assigned stores. I also helped set up new stores with the planning of store layouts and more.

Many times, I traveled around the country on the Supervalu® company jet to analyze stores that had major problems and give them tools to help them recover. I also helped set up new stores including two new Targets when meat was first introduced in their concept stores.

I also flew on the jets to research packing plants to help the company decide if we were going to buy products from the plant or not. I did that job for a decade. During my time on that job, I traveled outside the continental U.S., to the Virgin Islands, and Alaska.

After being a Meat Specialist, I became a Fresh Food Consultant. I worked with stores for three years the same way as meat specialist but covering all fresh departments in the stores including produce, bakery, deli's, and meat.

Heart Surgery

I accepted a Supervalu® Merchandising position working in the office again for the last seven years of my career. I wrote ads and managed the Fort Wayne Indiana division meat department from our Hopkins, Minnesota office.

In 2017 I had open heart surgery. My mitral valve was leaking causing me to have many dizzy spells and trouble walking at times. Once again it was a great success, and I was able to go back to work.

Just before I had heart surgery, my mother at age 86 passed away. That was a tremendous loss.

Supervalu® was sold to a company called UNFI. After a few months, their ownership started laying off a lot of staff. I was one.

I decided it was time to retire instead of drawing unemployment. I just did not want to go looking for another job at that point in my life.

It probably was a mistake as Covid hit and unemployment could have gone on for those years. But, I have no regrets as I have totally enjoyed my retirement without all the job stresses I had before.

Ladder Splatter

I was doing some construction work that required a beam to support the upstairs floor joists above the garage floor eight feet below. The beam (sixteen-and-a-half feet long, twelve inches wide, and four inches thick) needed to be lifted up eight feet with ends supported on the floor. I do not remember how heavy the beam was--somewhere between 250 to 300 pounds.

As I was working, my two kids were helping me by bringing tools I needed for the project. I had my kids stand away from me and the beam while I was putting the beam in place.

I lifted one end up and had it on a support. I moved my step ladder near the other end of the beam. As I was walking the beam's other end up the ladder, and almost on the support, my ladder legs gave way. The ladder, with extra weight and force, obviously could not support my weight plus movement with the beam.

Once again, somehow, by what I believe to be guardian angles, I was able to keep the beam away from falling on my kids. The accident only broke my wrist bone as the beam came crashing down.

Fall and Shatter

After retiring and moving to Nevada, I planned to do more shop projects, bike riding, and kayaking. Before I could really do all that, I needed to get my garage organized. One of the first projects was getting tools and shelves setup.

One thing when moving from a family home (Cottage Grove, MN) to a retirement house (Henderson, NV) was space consideration. Our Minnesota home had a sixteen-by-ten foot stand-alone workshop for my tools. Plus, our two-stall garage held bikes, kayak, fishing rods, and a lot more.

In our new two-stall garage, I had to use all the space possible—up to its ten-foot ceiling. With that in mind, some items needed to be high on the wall to get it all to fit in and be organized. One day, around my truck, were both our three-wheel bikes, and many other items scattered around the floor.

I hopped up onto my tall (3' 6") workbench to hang some items high on the wall when I stumbled and fell off the bench. Doing my best not to fall on one of the bikes I landed on just one foot shattering my heel while falling over the bike into my truck. At age sixty-five, it was truly a miracle that I did not break more than I did.

The moral of this story: when moving, ensure there is plenty of room if climbing a ladder onto a bench. This mishap incapacitated me for six months. I think other than the Pearl-Gate, and open heart surgery, this incidents was the third longest period I was laid up.

Children Became Adults

When we moved from Bismarck to the Twin Cities, it was really hard on my kids. After the first year they were very happy we made them move.

Kayla attended University of St. Thomas in St. Paul, Minnesota where she received a bachelor's degree in biology and later was awarded a master's degree at Perdue University in Fort Wayne, Indiana where she met Nick, her husband.

After graduation and wedding, Kayla and Nick moved to Birmingham, Alabama where she received her doctorate (PhD) in biology. She is now The Chair of Physical and Life Sciences at Nevada State University in Henderson, Nevada.

Kayla and Nick gave us two beautiful grandchildren, Sadie, now nine-years-old, and Odin who is seven.

Wade was very much involved in sports throughout high school, especially basketball and football.

After high school, he was accepted into Gustavas Adolphus College in Saint Peter, Minnesota where he played both basketball and football. While there, Wade received his Bachelor of Arts (BS) degrees in Geography and History.

He then went to the University of Arizona in Tuson and received his Master of Science degree in Planning. He met his wife Carla there. Now they live in San Francisco, California where they both work for the city of San Francisco--Wade in transportation planning and Carla in city planning.

Dream

Jeanne and I never dreamed that our kids would have had the opportunities they did from our very humble beginning.

As many retirees do, Jeanne and I moved to Henderson, Nevada to be near our grandchildren. We enjoy seeing them growing up and seeing all the opportunities kids have these days. It is absolutely amazing, and we love it.

Postscript

Thanks to all who pushed me to get writing. Especially my son, Wade, and my brother, Gary, who were the biggest influences on me to do so.

Most of all, I dearly thank my wife Jeanne for putting up with me for the past forty-three years and supporting me in every aspect of my life.

Other GWW Books:

https://www.RelatingToAncients.com/

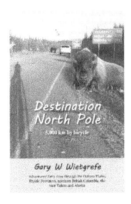

Printed in the USA
CPSIA information can be obtained
at www.ICGtesting.com
JSHW012129071024
71140JS00004B/11